SANA'A
City of Contrast

SANA'A
City of Contrast

Photographs by

Rosalie Rakow

Text by

Lynda J. Rose

Transliteration

Every attempt has been made to keep the transliteration in this text as simple as possible. There is no distinction between the long and short vowels or diphthongs, nor between the multiple sounds of the Arabic consonants. The definite article is always written as "al," regardless of case or elision, and the feminine "ö" is written "ah." Both the regular and irregular plural forms are indicated by adding the English "s" or "es."

The anglicized spelling of well-known words, such as Yemen, Mecca and Koran, has been used for easier recognition, though they do not conform to the basic transliteration system.

A short glossary appears at the end of the text.

Copyright © 1981 by Rosalie Rakow and Lynda J. Rose

All rights reserved including the right to reproduce this book or parts thereof in any form.

Library of Congress Catalog Card Number: 81-81195
ISBN 0-9606244-2-2

Printed in the United States of America

Published by
Tandem Publishers
5821 Banning Place
Burke, Virginia 22015 U.S.A.

Acknowledgments

The photographer and author wish to express their gratitude to the following persons for their help:

Al Qadi Ismail al Akwaa
Larry Bartlett
Nancy Coats
Barbara Croken
Edward Gnehm
Hassan Mohamed al Haifi
Mouna Hashem
Patricia Hedetniemi
John T. Hedetniemi
Betsy Lane
Ambassador George Lane
Jan Mandaville
Carlyn McManus
Etienne Renaud
Abdulaziz Saqaf

With special thanks to our husbands, Jim Rakow and John Rose, whose support and understanding made this book possible

Dedicated to
the people of Sana'a

Exhibits from the National Museum photographed with the permission of al Qadi Ismail al Akwaa, Director of Antiquities and Libraries, Sana'a, Yemen Arab Republic

Map of nineteenth-century Sana'a by Renzo Manzoni obtained from the Ministry of Public Works, Sana'a, Yemen Arab Republic

In the nineteenth century Sana'a, with two main walled areas, was in the shape of a figure eight with gates linking the twin sectors to the central Mutawwakil.

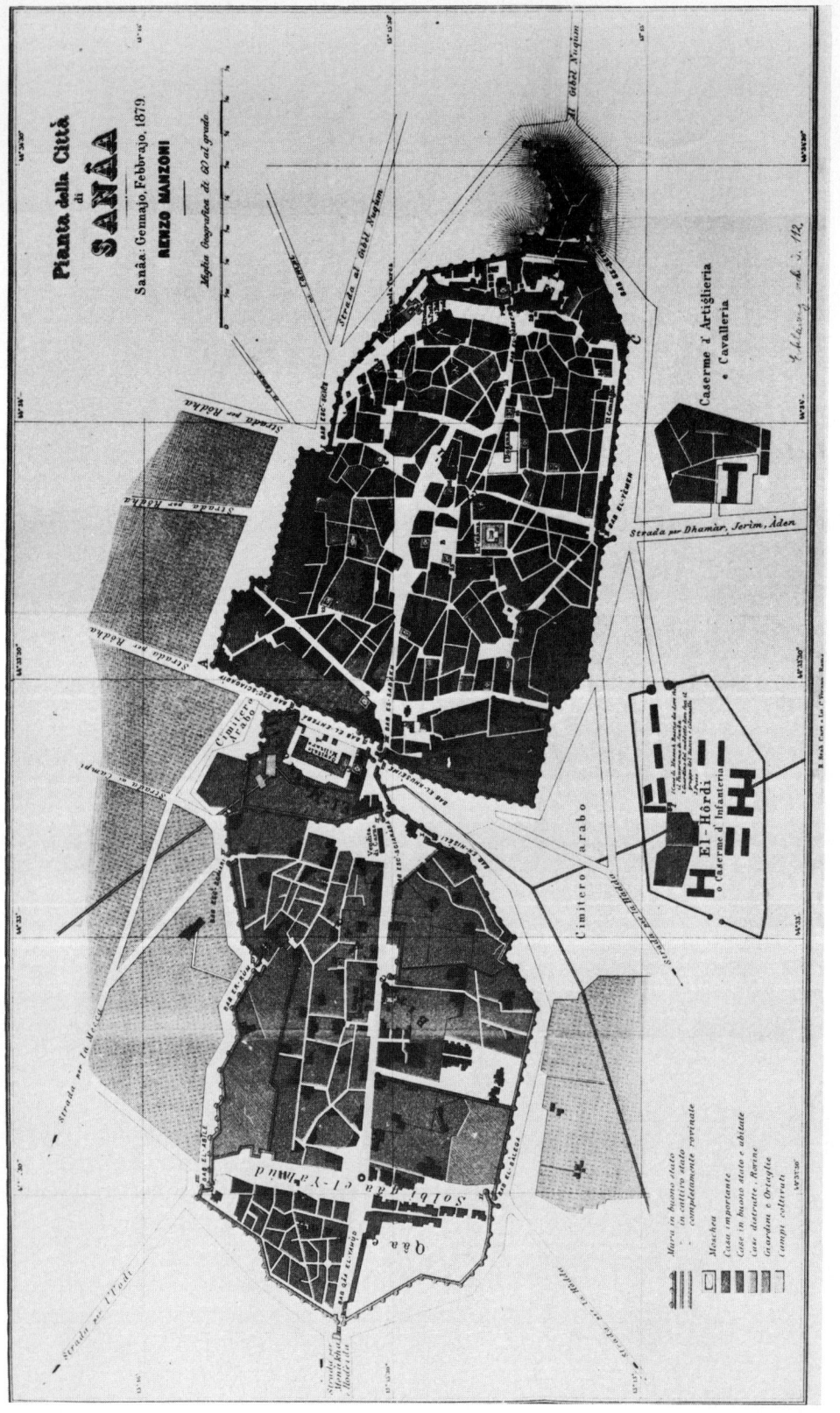

Introduction: Sana'a Through the Centuries

The Sam City Hotel in downtown Sana'a is named in honor of the son of Noah, endorsing a local legend that Sam was the founder of the city. This would, as some scholars claim, give Sana'a, capital of the Yemen Arab Republic, the distinction of being the oldest living city in the world. However, in absence of extensive archaeological excavations, the city's exact age is unknown, and its role in the flourishing civilizations of Arabia Felix remains an intriguing collection of legends, poetic descriptions and speculation.

Archaeologists can affirm that Sana'a existed several centuries before Islam as a commercial center, situated as it is along the trade route from Aden to Mecca, and that it was a seat of government under Jewish, Christian and pagan kings. Many claim that it may also have been a place of religious pilgrimage.

The Sana'a of pre-Islamic days was centered around the site of the present citadel, east of the Old Town. The shops and *samsarah*s were in a depression on the western edge, outside the original walls, which were much higher than those surrounding the Old Town in later centuries. Five gates led into the city, each protected by front sentry towers, and there was a sentry walk along the top of the wall.

Arabic literature extols a legendary Ghamdan Palace, a twenty-story skyscraper built on the rise now occupied by the citadel. The home of Himyarite kings, the palace was a magnificent structure of marble, brass and granite. It had a fine alabaster roof and, from each of its four corners, a hollow brass lion roared in the wind.

In what was then the center of the town, the Christian Abyssinians built a cathedral, al-Qalis, in the middle of the sixth century. The church, built to rival Mecca as a religious shrine, was adorned with precious stones and painted wood carvings, and the brilliant marble dome, protected by a cloak, was only uncovered on feast days.

When Islamic armies were sweeping the world in the seventh century, the tribesmen of Yemen were among early converts to the new religion, and the Great Mosque, built during the time of the Prophet Muhammad, is the most ancient Islamic monument still in existence. Some of the pillars and inscriptions in the mosque are pre-Islamic and may, along with some sculptures and ornaments, have been re-used from al-Qalis or Ghamdan Palace, both of which were evidently destroyed before its construction. The Great Mosque, repeatedly damaged by floods and sackings, has been rebuilt and enlarged many times, and in the twelfth and thirteenth centuries, the eastern section, the minarets, and the wooden ceilings were added. The small square domed construction in the courtyard, resembling the *ka'bah* in Mecca, was built in 1600 by the Ottomans.

In the early Middle Ages, Sana'a suffered invasion and pillaging, at times almost falling into ruin as tribes, dynasties and foreign powers struggled for rule. However, by the twelfth century, the city had grown in a westerly direction to the *sailah*. A Jewish quarter grew up within the walls on the eastern bank of the riverbed, and a small settlement developed outside the northern gate, Bab Shu'ub, around the tomb of one of the Prophet's companions. Between the *sailah* and the Jewish quarter, palaces and large houses were built in what became known as the Bustan al-Sultan quarter. The gardens and mosques surrounding these dwellings were watered by an ingenious system of underground canals which crossed the town from south to north.

At two separate periods of history, the Turks occupied most of Yemen and ruled from Sana'a. The Golden Age of the Ottoman Empire had a great influence on the city's architecture, and all the mosques with domes and minarets either date from the occupations or added these features during those times. The Bakiliyah Mosque on the eastern wall of the Old Town is one of the most prominent Turkish mosques in the city, with its domes of graduated sizes and its inscribed columns. Residents of Sana'a still use the many Turkish baths, of which the most famous are the Maidan across from the citadel, and the Sultan along the western bank of the *sailah*. Other reminders of the Ottoman presence include the two-story barracks on the southern side of the city and many government buildings in the western sector.

In the late seventeenth century the Jews established a new settlement at the western edge of Bir al-'Azab, one and a half kilometers from the Old Town. Between this settlement and the ancient city, a Turkish quarter developed along 'Abd al-Nasir Street, a residential area of palaces and gardens. These were interspersed with scattered groups of dwellings belonging to peasants, craftsmen and merchants, built directly on the street with gardens and orchards in the courtyards behind them.

A walled palace complex, the Mutawwakil, was erected in the first half of the eighteenth century between the Old Town and the Turkish quarter. This complex consisted of two palaces, a mosque, a bath house and a large garden with a *mafraj* tower on the northern edge.

During their second occupation, the Turks built a wall around the western section of the city, not as high as that of the Old Town and without a sentry walk. Its western gate marked the start of the road to al-Hudaidah. Thus Sana'a, with two walled areas, was in the shape of a figure eight with the Mutawwakil in the center. A total of ten gates led into the city.

During the modernization of the past two decades, much of the Mutawwakil and large sections of all the walls have been destroyed.

In the following pages, we will examine Sana'a as it exists today—a city integrating twentieth-century concepts and customs with a rich and ancient heritage. We hope our photographs, descriptions of the physical and sociological aspects of Sana'a, and brief portraits of some of its citizens will serve as an introduction to this unrenowned, yet interesting city.

Sana'a Museum: A Sabaean inscription (850–115 B.C.) in limestone describes the building method used to construct a six-story house, very similar to the method still used in Yemen today. Found in Zafar.

Nestled below the peak of Jabal Nukum, Sana'a retains a medieval appearance which contrasts sharply to its recent surge into the twentieth century.

Sana'a, City of Contrast

Sana'a, capital of the Yemen Arab Republic, is an oasis amidst the rugged Sarat Mountains along the southern tip of the Arabian peninsula. Nestled on a fertile plateau at an altitude of 2,400 meters, the city has a perfect climate—long summers of warm, sunny days and cool, clear evenings, and mild winters with brisk nights. The humidity is very low and, at certain times of the year, a layer of dust hazes the horizon and the wind sends twisting dust devils sweeping across the plain. Despite little rainfall, the fields surrounding Sana'a are green with apricot trees, almond and walnut groves, and bushes of *qat*, the mildly-euphoric leaf chewed daily by many Yemenis.

The oldest living city in Yemen, Sana'a has existed since at least 540 A.D. In the years before Islam, it was already the home of kings, who dwelt in the towering Ghamdan Palace and worshiped in a splendid marble-domed cathedral built in the center of the ancient town. Caravans of spices, incense and balsam journeyed northward from its *samsarah*s, returning to fill the bustling markets with silk, indigo, brass and silver.

Sana'a, capital of the Yemen Arab Republic. At an altitude of 2,400 meters in the Sarat mountain range of central Yemen, the city is one of the highest capitals in the world.

The houses of Sana'a are imposing monuments to the city's unique architectural design.

The pulse of the capital throbs most vibrantly in the
streets of the Old Town.

A modern office building on the outskirts of the capital is out of keeping with its surroundings. Shortly after its completion in 1980, a Design Review Board was established to insure that all future construction be more compatible with the traditional architectural style.

In the eighteenth century, European visitors to Sana'a described pillared temples and sumptuous palaces where *imam*s held court from silk dais in domed pavilions, and where gushing fountains watered fruit and flower gardens of every variety. Luring the traveler across the forbidding mountains and unrelenting deserts of Yemen, the remote, mystical city of Sana'a was eulogized the 'pearl of Arabia.'

The Yemen Arab Republic was established in 1962 and the gates of the capital city were thrown open to western technology and economic advancement. In only two decades modern industries, new buildings, paved roads teeming with traffic and shops filled with western merchandise have sprung up at an accelerating rate.

Yet, in sharp contrast to this modernization, the city retains an unspoiled medieval charm, created by a unique architectural design and a way of life essentially unchanged over the centuries. Here, 200,000 people with traditional customs of behavior, dress and daily routine dwell in an 'Arabian Nights' atmosphere of mosques, minarets, palaces, ancient walls and bazaars.

The adventurous visitor is still lured by an old Arab proverb, "Sana'a must be seen, even if the journey is long," and, for all those who come to know the city, there is a lasting fascination with its novelties, eccentricities, and contrasts, and with the friendly, gracious people who live there.

Through a Crumbling Mudbrick Wall...

For many centuries, the city of Sana'a was within a walled area which now lies in the eastern sector of the modern capital. Today the city has outgrown these walls, but the pulse of social and commercial activity still throbs vibrantly in the Old Town. The tide of its 60,000 inhabitants is swelled by a constant flow of tribesmen from outlying villages, shoppers from the western sector of the city, and tourists from other lands. They come to shop, exchange news and information, or simply to experience the beat of Sana'ani life.

It is here, in the labyrinth of markets, houses, *samsarah*s and mosques, threaded by a network of narrow lanes and open squares, that the contrasts of different eras are most dramatic. The ancient city succumbs to the impudent, haphazard intrusion of western civilization, and the visitor is baffled and amused by an eccentric hodge-podge of new and old.

Sana'a's Old Town is an authentic, living example of an ancient Islamic city.

Above: The approach to the Old Town along Zubairi Street passes the crumbling remains of the city's ancient mudbrick walls.

Below: The dry riverbed, or *sailah,* which borders the Old Town on the west is used as a major thoroughfare.

The approach to the Old Town along Zubairi Street is one of the most attractive sights in Sana'a. The eroding mudbrick wall, built to keep tribal marauders from a medieval trading town, now stretches brokenly around a dense, bustling metropolitan quarter. Above it rises an enchanting medley of brown, multi-storied buildings, the plaster tracery on their façades giving them an appearance of fantasy 'gingerbread' houses. Crowded together over centuries of reconstruction and expansion, their walls and rooftops rise in amiable irregularity to form meandering staircases in the sky.

Along the western side of the Old Town is the *sailah,* the riverbed for seasonal rainfall that flows from the mountains southeast of the city. In the droughts of recent years, cars and trucks have turned the *sailah* into a dusty, bumpy thoroughfare, but several times in the past its banks have overflowed, flooding the Old Town.

A wide street funnels into the Old Town from the area known as Bab Shu'ub, where formerly stood one of the five gates to the ancient city.

A traveling salesman auctions coats and jackets.

At the end of Zubairi Street is Bab al-Yemen, the only remaining gate of the original five into the Old Town. A two-way stream of pedestrians, automobiles, motorbikes and donkey carts pours through the wide stone arch, and its two large wooden doors, closed and barred at sunset each evening during the reign of the *imam*s, are now open day and night.

Both imported and locally-grown fruit and vegetables are available.

The *suq*, or market, begins just inside Bab al-Yemen, where a traveling salesman auctions coats and jackets and boys push wheelbarrows piled high with striped *futah*s and brass incense burners. Fruit and vegetables are sold here, along with imported items like chewing gum and candy, costume jewelry, scissors and flashlights, often by vendors whose only shop is a carpet spread beneath their wares. Sometimes an old man sits cross-legged, repairing milk gourds for the townswomen crouched around him. A traveling scissors-smith sharpens knives, scissors and *jambiyah*s on his foot-propelled grindstone. Always an old woman sells woven baskets, earthenware items, and straw brooms without handles. The rhythm of both Arabic and western music blares from booths displaying short-wave and transistor radios, cassette players and rows and rows of tapes.

When in season, many varieties of grapes are sold, whether from produce stands or from a peddler's single crate.

Old Town cobblers repair their clients' shoes, often resoling them with pieces of old tires.

Baskets woven in outlying villages are sold by veiled women.

A traveling scissors-smith sharpens knives, scissors and *jambiyah*s on his foot-propelled grindstone.

Veiled women carry large bundles on their heads as casually as westerners wear hats.

Board games are one of the favorite pastimes of Sana'ani youths.

Turbaned men in *futah*s and western jackets stroll singly or hand-in-hand with friends, the other hand resting proudly on the hilt of their *jambiyah*s. Some shuffle along, dwarfed under awkward loads of cardboard boxes or bulging burlap sacks. Others sun themselves on shop ledges, fingering prayer

Selling roasted lentils, a favorite Yemeni snack.

beads and gossiping with idle shopkeepers. The veiled women walk more purposefully, carrying everything on their heads—from large baskets of fruit or bread to twenty-liter cans of water balanced with one hand. Dark-eyed children are everywhere, tending their family's shop, darting through the crowded alleys, or playing board games in the open squares.

A pick-up truck loaded with firewood honks impatiently at a small herd of slow-moving goats and sheep. A fur-upholstered taxi inches past a laden camel and pedestrians step over a sleeping buffalo stretched across a tiny lane. Donkeys plod along, straddled by sacks of grain or harnessed to water carts ridden by boys who brandish a stick as an accelerator. An old woman sitting against a wall pulls her bare, *henna*-dyed feet out of the path of a careening motorcycle driven by a young man in western clothes and sunglasses.

The Old Town is an unpaved labyrinth of twisted lanes and narrow alleys.

Though pottery and stone vessels are the traditional cooking ware, aluminum pots and pans are also popular.

Tourists are enticed by antique shops—treasure troves of copperware, rifles, amber beads, bedouin jewelry, alabaster oil lamps and silver *jambiyah*s.

The streets soon fork and narrow into Suq al-Milh, where shops selling similar items are clustered together in quarters. Customers bargain for *jambiyah*s in antique silver filigree scabbards and for bedouin necklaces inlaid with semi-precious stones. There are gold bracelets and pendants, and strings of Red Sea coral and agate. Maria Theresa dollars, the currency of Yemen until 1964, are buried in piles of coins from other lands and times. Alabaster oil lamps, battered copper pots, and nineteenth century rifles from the United States, Britain, France and Turkey are especially prized by tourists.

The local residents admire colorful displays of Persian carpets, *mafraj* mattresses, fabric from southeast Asia, and painted metal suitcases from India. In Suq al-Halka there is a profuse selection of imported aluminum ware which is gaining popularity in Yemeni kitchens, but locally-made pottery and stone vessels are also available.

Grain merchants dip wheat, sorghum and lentils from woolen sacks and sell rock salt in wrappers made of plaited palm leaves.

Selling Yemen's excellent coffee, which is identified with the port of al-Mukha on the Red Sea. For hundreds of years Yemen monopolized the coffee market, and the term 'Mocha' is synonymous with high-quality coffee all over the world.

Spice and grain merchants dip wheat, sorghum and lentils from woolen sacks, coffee beans and husks from leather bags, and garlic bulbs, chillies and peppercorns from basket trays. Women in colorful *sitarah*s buy small quantities of cumin, ginger, cardamom and fenugreek, or plastic bags of raisins, fresh dates and almonds. Rock salt from the coastal area of Salif or the mines near Marib is sold in two-kilo sacks made of plaited palm leaves.

From their booths lined with old apothecary cabinets, vendors casually produce amber-colored myrrh and brown, woodeny frankincense, the famous resins of Arabia Felix. There are pieces of stone-like incense from India, crystals of white musk and tiny vials of thick, brown ambergris, which lend their distinctive odors to countless perfumes. There are also herbal plant compounds such as asafetida and aloe, still used by many home practitioners.

In one alleyway at noon, the shops are mobbed by men clutching wads of *riyal*s which they eagerly exchange for bunches of *qat*, in anticipation of an afternoon spent chewing the euphoric leaves and socializing.

A crowded *suq* **where customers come daily to bargain for fresh** *qat,* **a mildly euphoric leaf chewed by many Yemenis each afternoon for entertainment and relaxation.**

Wads of *riyal*s, sometimes amounting to as much as US $60, are exchanged for an afternoon's supply of *qat*.

To insure freshness the choicest *qat* sprigs are wrapped in banana leaves.

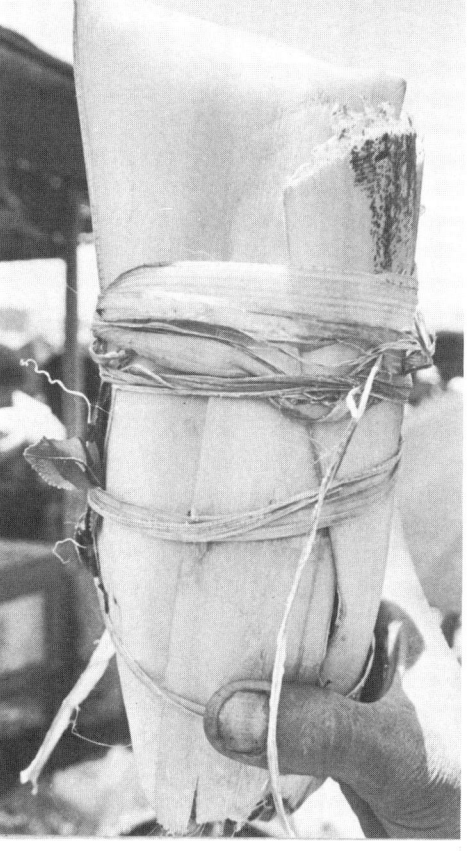

The quality and freshness of the *qat*, which is trucked into the city daily from nearby fields, determine the price, which ranges from twenty-five to three hundred *riyal*s for one person's afternoon supply.

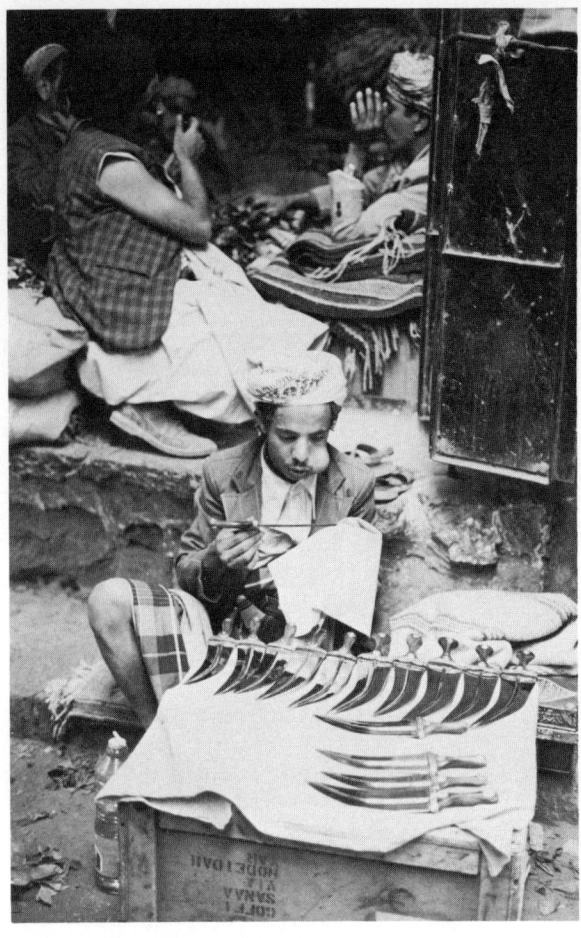

This peddler is chewing the *qat* leaves, swallowing the juice and packing the pulp into his cheek.

Behind the hardware *suq*, narrow alleys are lined with tiny workshops where age-old crafts are still practised.

Pieces are cut from discarded automobile tires to make sturdy buckets or soles for leather sandals.

Many crafts, including that of blacksmith, have been passed down through generations of the same family.

Behind the hardware *suq*, with its multitude of fixtures and implements, is a seldom-explored maze of thinner lanes lined with tiny workshops. Here, the age-old crafts of the blacksmith, the carpenter and the locksmith are still in evidence, practised on the same spot by succeeding generations of the same families for hundreds of years. Deafening blows ring out as red-hot steel is pounded into picks, hammers and axes. Window frames and cabinets are built in the lane in front of cluttered carpentry shops, and locksmiths fashion metal locks and ten-inch keys for Sana'ani homes.

Many Old Town craftsmen still rely on tools, such as this wooden drill, which were designed centuries ago.

A carpenter shapes wooden mounts for door knockers.

Making oversized wooden locks for Sana'ani homes and shops...

... which require keys of equal proportions.

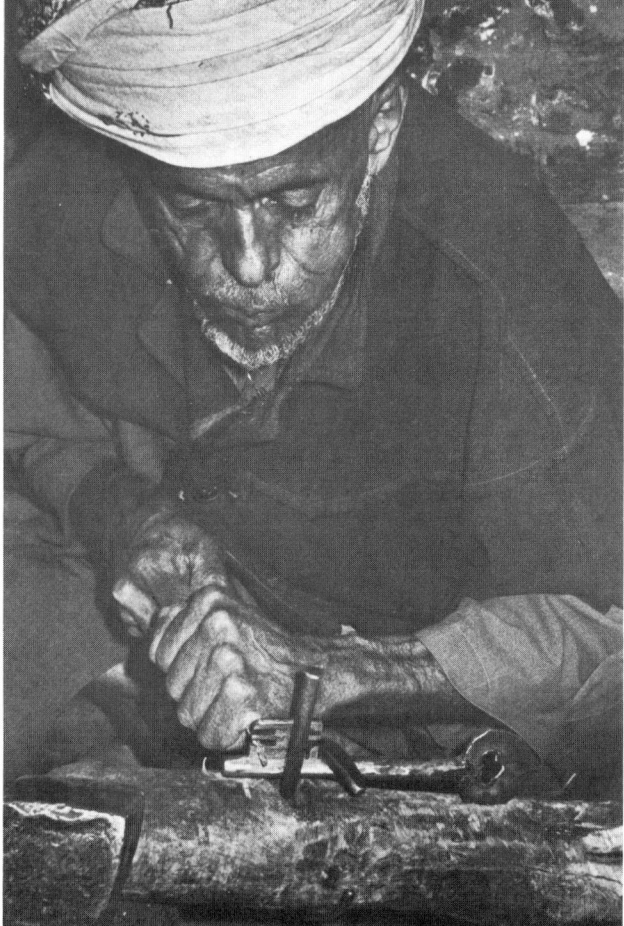

The production of the *jambiyah* **is the most esteemed craft in the Old Town and there are many stages in its construction. Here, the hand-carved hilt is studded with copper wire.**

Jambiyah blades are fused to their hilts with boiling pitch and polished to a brilliant shine.

The most esteemed and profitable craft is the making of *jambiyah*s, the distinctive curved daggers worn by Yemeni men since ancient times. Even today a well-polished, expensive *jambiyah* is a sign of social status and wealth, and is worn by Sana'ani men on special occasions if not daily.

Yemen has long been renowned for its production of high-quality steel and at one time sharp weapons from the land of Arabia Felix were famous throughout the world. Today, however, the forged blades are imported from Japan and Italy. Otherwise, the construction of the *jambiyah* has not changed in centuries.

Mounting circular seals or coins on the *jambiyah* hilt.

The value of the *jambiyah* depends on the quality of the hilt, and craftsmen carve the most extravagant ones from rhinoceros horn which, with age, takes on the deep luster of amber. The carved hilts are washed and polished with ash, and pieces of copper wire are hammered in for decoration. Circular seals or coins are mounted on the hilt after it is fused to the polished blade with boiling pitch.

After being bound with strips of goatskin the *jambiyah* sheaths will be hung on embroidered or leather belts.

The various styles of the *jambiyah* reflect a wide range of quality and workmanship.

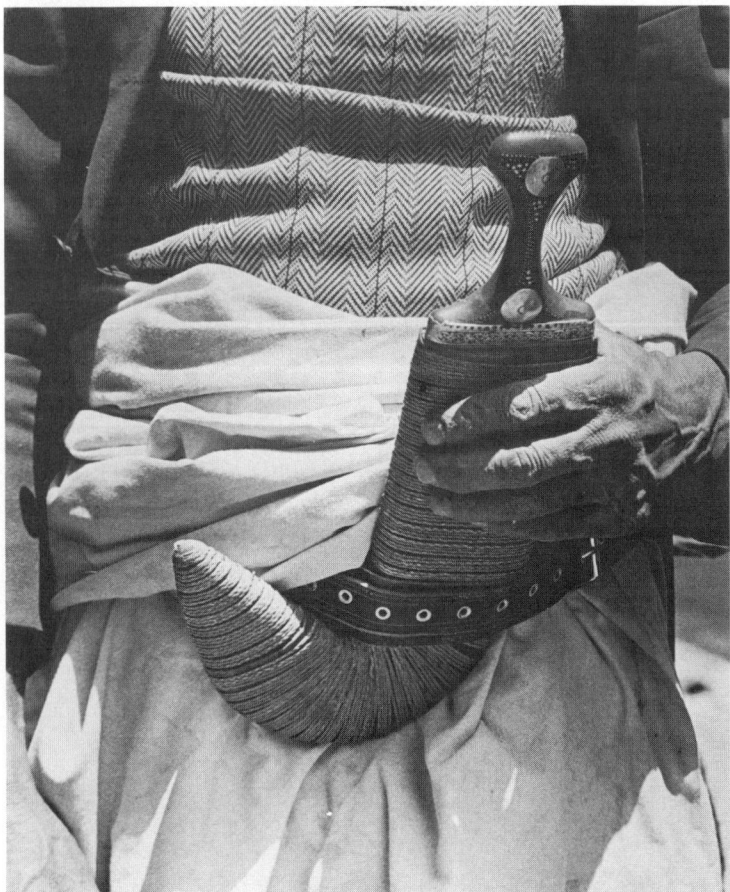

Formerly, most *jambiyah*s were encased in silver filigree scabbards which are, today, very expensive. Conventional wooden ones are made by carving two wide J-shapes from soft white wood, hollowing them to fit around the blade, and binding them together with strips of goatskin. The finished knife is usually mounted on a leather belt, though some are on intricately embroidered or woven cloth.

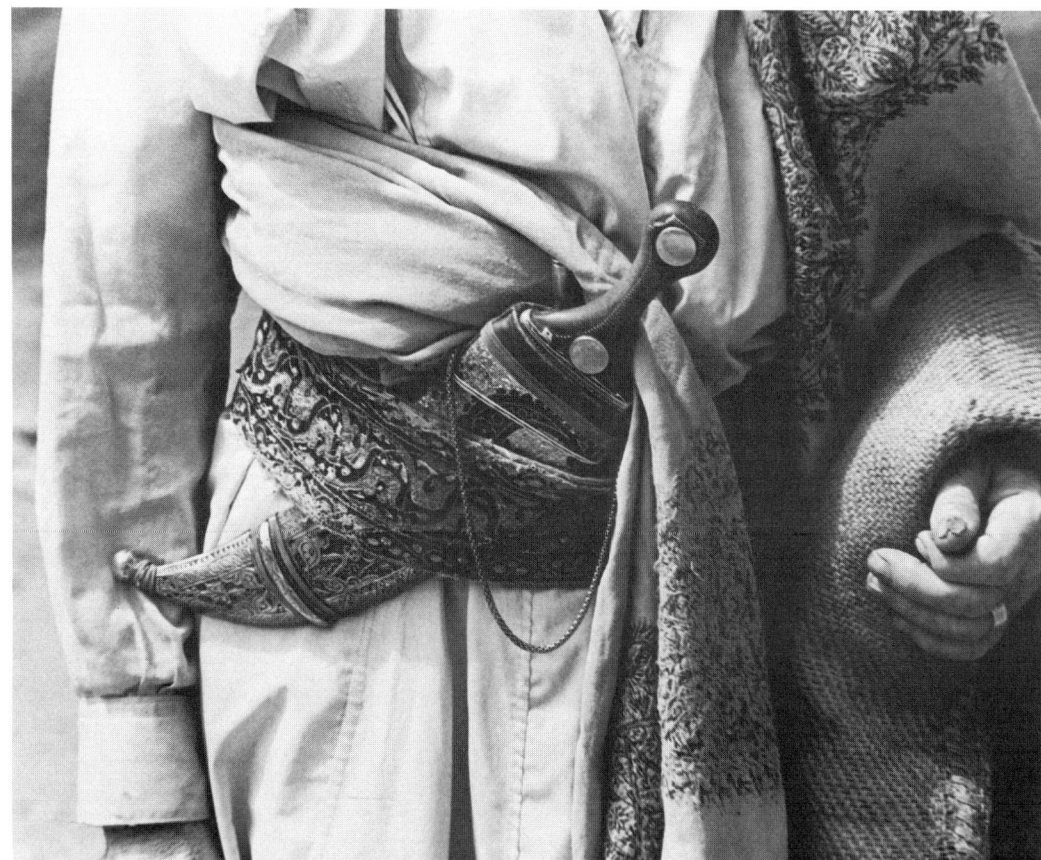

Most activity slackens in the afternoon as shopkeepers and craftsmen relax with their *qat* and/or waterpipe.

In the afternoon, the bustle of the Old Town becomes less intense. As their customers disappear, shopkeepers who remain open begin to chew *qat* or smoke the *mada'ah*. The craftsmen work on, but they, too, pause regularly to select a handful of choice leaves, laid carefully out of reach of flying sparks. One old blacksmith lays his hammer aside periodically to grind *qat* for his toothless gums. Another craftsman, determined not to miss a puff, suspends the mouthpiece of his waterpipe at face level between his layers of shirts. Nearby there is a pottery jug of water, often infused with incense, to quench the smoker's thirst and to offset the bitterness of the *qat* leaves.

A *samsarah*, one of the ancient inn-warehouses used since the time of the spice caravans. The brick walls of the *samsarah*s are decorated with relief diamond shapes and arches.

Interspersed among the single-level stalls and workshops of the market area are several multi-storied *samsarah*s, or caravanserais. Most of these *samsarah*s are very old (one dates from the fourteenth century) and are remnants of the days when caravans of myrrh, frankincense, and spices passed through Sana'a on their way to the Mediterranean. The traders paid taxes to the territories they crossed, and in turn were granted lodging for the night, provisions for the next stage of their journey and, hopefully, safe conduct. In Sana'a the goods were weighed and inspected and the tax paid at the Samsarat al-Mizan in the center of the market. Merchandise destined for the city was transferred on the backs of porters to other *samsarah*s for storage. Ongoing caravans were also lodged in the *samsarah*s, the travelers sleeping on the upper floors and their animals in the stables below.

Today the caravans come no more, and the *samsarah*s, especially the upper levels, are beginning to fall into ruin. Some, still retaining their enormous balance scales, continue to serve as warehouses and inspection stations, their arched courtyards and pillared galleries piled high with sacks of coffee, wheat and spices. Formerly owned by rich merchants, they are now mostly endowed to the Ministry of Awqaf, which uses the income derived from these and other properties to maintain the mosques and help the poor.

In several dark stables of the Old Town sesame oil used for cooking and in medicine is extracted by the ancient method of mortar and pestle. A blindfolded camel walks in a circle, grinding seeds into the costly oil.

Away from the dense, bustling markets, quieter lanes lead to the brown mudbrick houses of the Old Town.

Window boxes with wooden lacework allow women to peer through the closed shutters without being seen.

Away from the market of shops and *samsarahs*, overlooking wider lanes and open squares, are the brown mudbrick tower houses of the Old Town. Despite the forbidding walls around the houses, life here is very communal, and the rutted lanes and cul-de-sacs of the residential areas are usually bustling with activity. Through low doorways, one can peep into small treeless courtyards, landscaped in

These women in *sitarah*s have thrown back the *maghmuq* to reveal their inner face veil, the *lithmah*.

Women who appear veiled in the streets wear either the black *sharshaf* or the colorful *sitarah*.

rock and dust. Here, veiled women in long-sleeved, full-skirted dresses, only their eyes visible between the folds of the black *lithmah*, gossip in the morning sun, while bare-bottomed babies play in the dirt at their feet. Men break up gnarled limbs for firewood, or share a glass of tea with their companions. A tourist is immediately surrounded by dark-haired children, their games of marbles, hopscotch, or jumprope readily abandoned. Plump toddlers, their perfect complexions greyed by dust, stare intently at the camera, and boys with spidery legs strike audacious poses. Little girls in brocade dresses, trousers and jewelry hold up *henna*-painted hands for visitors to admire. Older girls wrap their shawls around their faces and dart into the shadows, their lively brown eyes wide and teasing.

The children of the Old Town, shy, ...

... curious, ...

... mischievous, ...

. . . and intent.

Scattered among the streets and houses, an integral part of life in the Old Town, are over forty mosques, the place of prayer, meeting, and meditation for Muslims. Amidst the vibrancy of everyday life, they are calm, sobering reminders of the strict Islamic tenets to which most Sana'anis adhere.

The Bakiliyah Mosque on the eastern wall of the Old Town was built during the first Turkish occupation of Yemen in the sixteenth century.

One of the forty mosques scattered among the streets and houses, all an integral part of life in the Old Town.

Many of the mosques in the Old Town are simple, walled structures with an open courtyard containing facilities for ablutions. Around these are large prayer galleries with flat roofs. An arched niche in the wall indicates the direction of Mecca, which all worshipers face to pray. The Friday sermon is delivered from a pulpit approached by a carved wooden staircase. Formerly illuminated by alabaster lamps which burned sesame oil or candles, the mosques are now lit by electric bulbs, and the floor is covered with locally-made or Persian carpets on which the congregation kneels to pray. The call to prayer is made five times a day by the *mu'adhdhin* through speakers on the roof of the mosque.

The arched galleries of the Great Mosque.

The most impressive mosque in the Old Town is al-Jami' al-Kabir, the Great Mosque, with its minarets, white arches, and pre-Islamic pillars. This is the mosque usually visited by Old Town male residents for Friday prayer. Its wooden ceilings are carved in floral patterns and inscribed with Koranic verses. Beyond the three rows of arches in each gallery, the curtained doors lead to the courtyard dominated by a square domed structure resembling the *ka'bah* in Mecca. The outer walls of the mosque contain stones bearing pre-Islamic inscriptions, and on the northern wall there is a special door originally for the use of the *imam,* now reserved for important government officials. The library on the upper floor of al-Jami' al-Kabir contains ancient handwritten texts on history, religion and medicine, mostly from the private collection of the *imam*s.

Before the introduction of public schools, scholars studied, worked and wrote in the mosques. The library of the Great Mosque contains handwritten manuscripts (some a thousand years old) on history, religion, agriculture and medicine.

Some of the money used to support the mosques of Sana'a comes from the market gardens of the Old Town. Always below street level, these small green oases in a city devoid of any free-growing shrubs and flowers are best viewed from the roofs of houses and nearby *samsarah*s. The tenant farmers who work them plant almond trees and crops of tomatoes, onions and lettuce, which, if a mosque is nearby, are irrigated with water from ablutions.

Pre-Islamic pillars were re-used in building the original section of the Great Mosque.

The interior of al-Maidan, one of the public Turkish bath houses in Sana'a. Having proceeded through a succession of hot and temperate rooms, the bather relaxes and cools down here before leaving the bath house.

In the Old Town there are at least fifteen Turkish bath houses, their low roofs topped by numerous small domes. Most men and women of Sana'a visit the *hammam* three or four times a week to wash away the heat and dust of the city, and to insure a state of cleanliness before prayer. Friday, the busiest day, is reserved for men preparing for the important end-of-week sermon and worship. For a small fee, the bather undergoes a ritual of sweating, rubbing and dousing in a succession of warm and hot rooms. He emerges refreshed and cleansed, ready for prayer.

The walls of the Old Town are slowly crumbling, and capitulation to the twentieth century steadily becomes more imminent. The human voice, former clarion of these narrow alleys, is muffled by the sudden thrusts of motorcycles, the blasts of car horns, and the roar of airplanes overhead. Men and women in western dress are not the rarity they were a few years ago and aerosol cans, colored plastic bags, and flattened cigarette cartons clutter the lanes. Nevertheless the Old Town remains, for the moment, an anachronism in today's modern world, a place where medieval convention and ageless simplicity prevail.

The century-old portal of Bab al-Yemen is mounted with wooden doors, one of which was penetrated by a cannonball during the civil war of 1962–69. Before the war the doors were closed and barred at sunset each evening.

The century-old military citadel on a rise outside the eastern edge of the Old Town is believed to be on the site of the legendary Ghamdan Palace, the first skyscraper mentioned in history.

Stones bearing Himyaritic inscriptions (115 B.C. - 525 A.D.) have been re-used over the centuries. These examples were discovered in the wall of a house in a cul-de-sac in the Old Town.

Located in the eastern quarter of the Old Town, this man-high circular wall marks the site of al-Qalis, a Christian cathedral built in the middle of the sixth century.

A drinking cistern which formerly was at the gate of Bab al-Yemen now stands half a kilometer away beside a narrow alley in the western part of the Old Town. It was built during the reign of Imam Yahya in the early 1900's and is inscribed with the Muslim profession of faith.

Al-Hajj Ali

Al-Hajj Ali has been a *shaikh* for fourteen years. He was elected by the people of his quarter as adviser, judge, and to represent them in the city government. A graduate of a religious secondary school, Ali wears the robe, turban and shawl of a holy, learned man of Sana'a. He walks with a cane, his beard is yellowed with age, and tight grey curls peep from beneath his turban. However, his lively brown eyes and sparkling good humor discount his sixty-odd years, and he is a popular and beloved figure in his neighborhood.

Ali explains that the duties of a *shaikh* include collecting taxes, sealing marriage contracts and acting as mediator and judge in civil cases, especially divorce.

Sana'ani husbands can divorce their wives for virtually any reason by simply stating "I divorce you" three separate times in the presence of two witnesses. A man provides for his estranged wife according to the terms of their marriage contract, which often means she is dependent on her own or her family's resources. If he divorces his wife for infidelity or disobedience, a husband is not required to support her at all.

Women can only seek a divorce from their husbands if permission to do so is written in the marriage contract. The divorce is granted at the discretion of the *shaikh*, usually only in extreme cases of physical abuse, non-support, sexual neglect or impotence. If the wife is successful in convincing the *shaikh* to give her a divorce, no support from the husband is required, and, in fact, the *mahr* is returned to him. If the marriage contract does not permit her to initiate a divorce, the only recourse open to an unhappy wife is to return to her father's house and hope that her husband will seek a divorce.

Children are the property of their father and, though it is customary to leave daughters and very young sons with their mother, the father can claim them at any time. He will undoubtedly do so if the mother remarries, for it would be unthinkable for another man to rear one's children.

The divorce rate in Sana'a is very high and, though it presents many problems for women, an increasing number of them are taking the initiative in seeking divorces from their husbands. Ali was recently confronted by a young woman who wanted to work and, when her husband refused, decided to divorce him and support herself. Others, bored by the routine or disillusioned with their new household, are seeking independence to continue their schooling. Also, radio and television shows emphasizing love and personal happiness as integral features of daily life are changing the expectations women have for marriage.

"When I was a young man," says al-Hajj Ali, "life was simple, well-ordered, and a woman's role was to marry and raise a family. Now there are other alternatives, and we have women working in industries, government offices and banks. Yet parents, in an effort to protect the honor of the family, still marry their daughters off before the girls are old enough to know their own minds. It takes time to change old customs and ideas."

Meanwhile, Ali must decide between upholding the inveterate right of parents to arrange marriages for their children and granting unhappy girls the divorce they seek. Shaking his head bewilderedly, Ali complains, "It is not easy for an old *shaikh* like me to have to make such decisions."

...Into the Twentieth Century

Maidan al-Tahrir, or Liberation Square, is the heart of the western sector of Sana'a, junction of the Old Town and the newer quarters of the capital. Here, two hundred years ago, was built the Mutawwakil, a walled complex belonging to the royal family. It consisted of two palaces, a Turkish mosque, and a quaint circular tower crowned with a rectangular *mafraj*. The palaces were last used as royal residences by Imam Yahya, who lived in the Dar al-Sa'adah until 1948, and by his brother, governor of Sana'a, who lived in the Dar al-Shukr.

Today the gardens have disappeared, and the splendid buildings of the Mutawwakil stand amidst crowded tea shops, taxi stands and peddler carts. Dar al-Sa'adah is the governate of Sana'a and Dar al-Shukr houses the National Museum.

'Abd al-Mughni Street approaches the eighteenth century palace and former garden complex of the Mutawwakil.

Maidan al-Tahrir (Liberation Square), the junction of the Old Town and the newer western sector.

'Abd al-Mughni Street, which runs north-south behind Maidan al-Tahrir, was formerly an imposing suburban area between the Old Town and the Turkish quarter. Many shops and several hotels, including the modern Sam City and the multi-million dollar Sheba Hotel, are along 'Abd al-Mughni Street.

'Abd al-Nasir Street, also an important shopping area, connects Maidan al-Tahrir to al-Qa'a. Embassies and government ministries now occupy the old palaces, royal guest houses, and Turkish buildings adjoining the street.

The *mafraj* tower from which the royal family admired the former gardens of the Mutawwakil.

A wall built in the nineteenth century encircled Bir al-'Azab, the western section of the town, from Maidan al-Tahrir to the Jewish quarter in al-Qa'a. This quarter, built in the late seventeenth century and abandoned by Yemeni Jews emigrating to Israel in 1950, is reminiscent of the Old Town, with winding, rutted lanes, tiny shops and closely-built dwellings. Jewish houses, however, were not permitted to be higher than the old two-story minarets, nor to have exterior decorations, and the homes in al-Qa'a are built low around inner courtyards, their alabaster windows unadorned by tracery and arches.

There is a legend that the minarets of al-Jami' al-Mutawwakil were built low to prevent the *mu'adhdhin* from being distracted by royal women at the nearby palace windows.

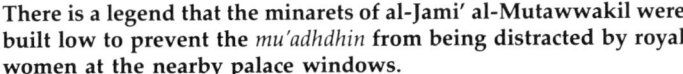

If one follows the few remaining stretches of the wall around Bir al-'Azab to the fine old sentry tower near the Mutawwkil, it is interesting to imagine the splendor it once encompassed. In this region, *imam*s and Turkish governors built sumptuous multi-storied palaces and country residences. The ground floor of the Turkish houses opened into rose gardens shaded by orange, cyprus and almond trees. There were gushing fountains and domed pavilions lined with silk cushions and Persian carpets.

The palaces of the Mutawwkil.

In the foreground stands the Dar al-Sada'ah, former residence of Imam Yahya and now the governate of Sana'a. In the background the tall building to the left of 'Abd al-Mughni Street is the Sam City Hotel, one of the first modern hotels built in the capital.

The National Museum, Dar al-Shukr, former residence of the governor of Sana'a.

View from the window seat of the National Museum.

The Yemeni palaces, such as Bait Abbass and al-Qasr al-Jumhuri, have top-floor *mafraj*es which overlooked the fertile gardens and orchards of Bir al-'Azab. Bait Abbass, with its unusual window seat, ornamented *mafraj*, and intricate colored windows, is today the Dar al-Hamd Palace Hotel. The President of Yemen hosts official receptions in al-Qasr al-Jumhuri, or Republican Palace.

Bait Abbass, which once belonged to the royal family, is now the Dar al-Hamd Palace Hotel. Its *mafraj* suite offers a panoramic view of the rapidly-growing western sector.

The President of Yemen hosts official receptions in al-Qasr al-Jumhuri (Republican Palace).

The Ministry of Health at Liberation Square was built during the second Turkish occupation and exemplifies Ottoman architecture.

Buildings of Egyptian design line 'Abd al-Mughni Street which runs north-south behind Maidan al-Tahrir.

Dar al-Bashair, a palace on Shara' al-Bawniyah, was the home of Crown Prince al-Badr. Upon the death of his father, Imam Ahmed, in September, 1962, al-Badr was appointed ruler. However, a week later revolutionists encircled and shelled the palace and al-Badr was forced to flee. Now, nearly hidden by walls and buildings, the home of the former prince is used for government offices.

Scribes set up office daily outside the mosque of the Mutawwakil.

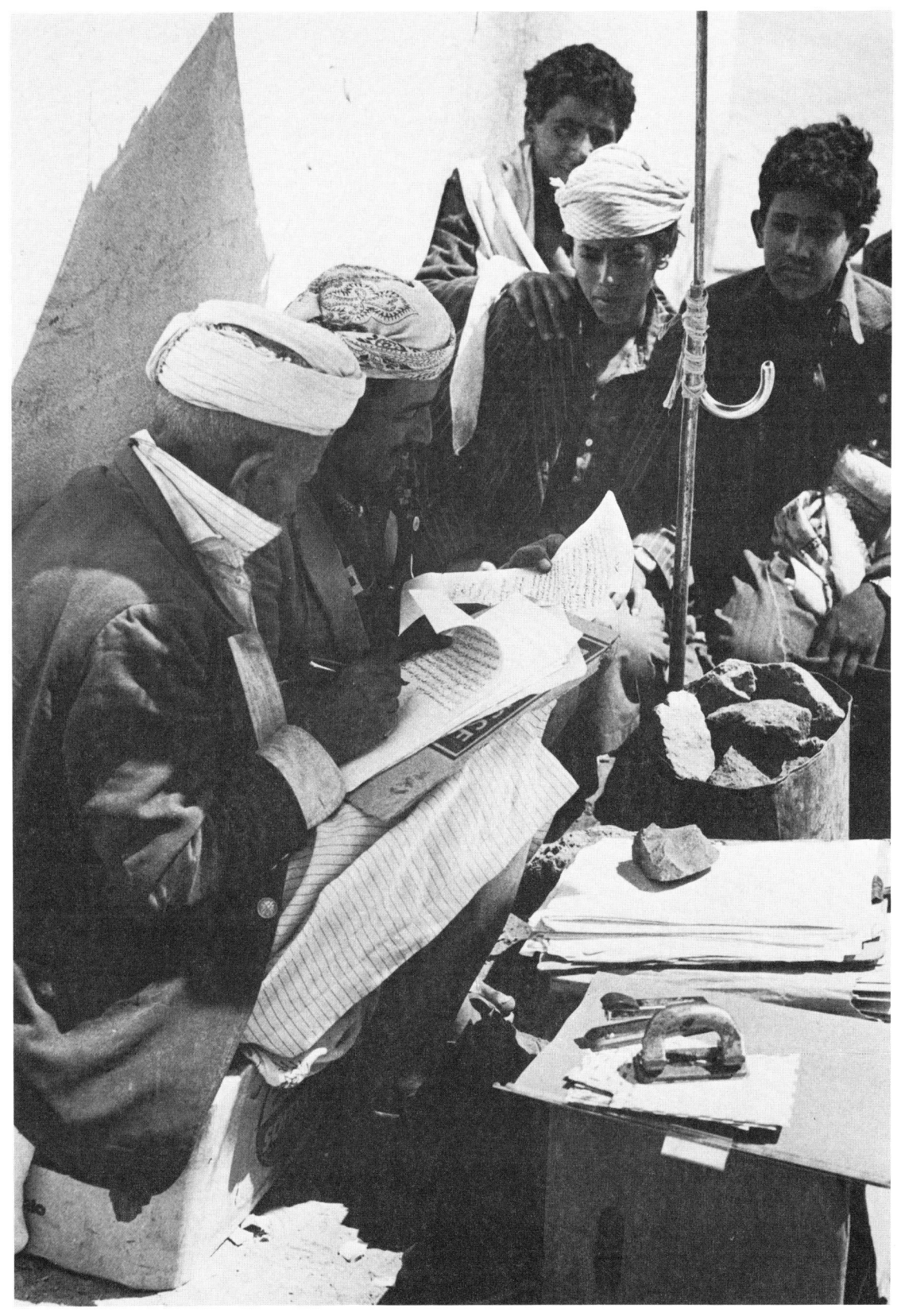

The beauty of many Sana'ani homes
approaches the splendor of the *imam*i palaces.

The Ministry of Justice on Wadi Dahr Road.

Commerce is the mainstay of Sana'a, and in the western sector the most recent entrepreneurs, the import retailers, operate on a full scale. In row shops large enough to permit customers inside, one can buy everything from perfume and refrigerators to Dutch cheese and tricycles. There are tailors, laundries, paint shops, furniture stores, and airline and travel agencies. Trim-waisted girls in *sharshaf* select gold bracelets and ready-made western dresses, and young men shop for cameras, transistor radios and digital watches.

Sana'a is a commercial city sustained by increasing consumer demands for imports, from Designer jeans to Casio calculators.

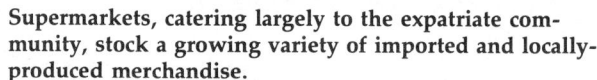

Supermarkets, catering largely to the expatriate community, stock a growing variety of imported and locally-produced merchandise.

Stone-oven bakeries sell hot fresh circles of wheaty *khubz,* and modern ones sell western loaves and pastries. Sidewalk cafes offer fruit milkshakes, plates of meat and vegetable stews, and spit-roasted chickens spiced with cumin, in competition with newly-opened fast food chains. *Qat* is sold fresh off the truck in an outlying shanty town of corrugated tin shacks and stalls.

The white-trimmed, mudbrick houses which characterize Sana'ani architecture.

The houses of Sana'a are reflections of an enduring pattern of life.

Years ago Old Town residents stepped up from cobblestone streets into their houses. Now, due to layers of gravel and dirt deposited in the roadways, many thresholds are a step below street level.

Crowded together over centuries of reconstruction and expansion, walls and rooftops rise to form meandering staircases in the sky.

Sana'ani men wear sports jackets, *futah*s **and turbans.**

The white gown, shawl and wrapped turban are the attire of holy, learned men.

Sana'anis often adorn their vehicles with tassels and trinkets, colored garlands and feathered plumes.

Men take care of household affairs, such as shopping, which require contact with people outside the family.

In the old quarters of the city life spills over into the narrow, unpaved streets. These women are whipping *hilbah* for the midday meal.

Behind the houses and shops of the western sector, gardens laid out in the late seventeenth century are still cultivated.

Tie-dying the invariable red and white patterns onto the *maghmuq*, the black outer veil worn with the *sitarah*.

Practising the new 'folk art' of Sana'a, welders fashion colorful iron gates which are used for shop fronts and in the entrances to walled residential compounds.

Weddings are celebrated by a week of bridal parties. On the day before the marriage the bride wears a new dress, her best jewelry and a colorfully-embroidered bridal veil.

Babies are welcome additions to Sana'ani families, regarded as gifts from Allah and assuring their mother of a preferred status in the household.

Some of the money used to support the mosques of Sana'a comes from market gardens, green oases wedged behind the brown walls of the Old Town.

A winding, unpaved lane in the Old Town.

Sidewalk vendors and their ever-changing displays line 'Abd al-Mughni Street.

A familiar street corner sight, these carts sell confections made of nuts, fruit, honey and sesame seed.

Above: Sana'a University from the ring road.

Below: The sports stadium behind the Sheba Hotel.

Sana'a Museum: A meter-high bronze statue of a notable found in Marib dates from 500–200 B.C.

Sana'a Museum: Exhibit of bridal wedding party. Woman in black is the bridal attendant. The Koran is in a purse on the wall above the bride's head, and eggs, flowers and candles in the room symbolize happiness and fertility.

Sana'a Museum: Throne of Imam Yahya, 1904–48.

The Great Mosque, built in the center of the Old Town in the seventh century (reputedly by order of the Prophet Muhammad), is the oldest Islamic monument in existence.

Women sell their round, flat loaves of homemade bread.

Traditional wheat bread is also made in stone-oven bakeries.

The streets of the western sector are wider than those of the Old Town, and the main ones are paved. Donkey carts, motorcycles and bicycles weave among all makes of Japanese, European and American cars, and an occasional herd of goats stops traffic. Water trucks make deliveries from wells outside the city, refrigerated trucks bring imported frozen food from the port of al-Hudaidah, and pickups haul day laborers to their worksites. The city's few traffic lights are augmented by white-uniformed policemen, and newspaper boys haunt the busiest intersections. Early in the morning, the gutters are swept by shawled women and bare-legged boys bent over brooms and wheelbarrows.

The periodicals of many foreign nations are available at local newsstands.

On the unpaved, rock-strewn side streets, old men and veiled women grumble when passing cars raise a cloud of dust. Children play in sand and gravel piled on new construction sites and, nearby, goats, cats and chickens browse patiently for food. The streets are brown and barren, though an occasional willowy branch dangles over a wall, whispering of carefully-nurtured plants and trees in secluded gardens.

Each day sidewalk rotisseries sell hundreds of spit-roasted chickens spiced with cumin.

Several fast food chains have opened in Sana'a.

Tea shops are popular social gathering places for men.

As the capital has launched an intense effort toward modernization, a full-scale building boom has completely ignored the boundary of the old walls. Both the Arab and Jewish cemeteries, once on the outskirts of the original developments, are now built over. Outlying villages such as Safiyah and al-Jiraf have been engulfed as residential suburbs and commercial areas have sprung up desultorily. The rounded corners and crumbling walls of the remaining mudbrick houses look out of place and neglected, and everywhere there are random triangles and slivers of unusable land, squeezed out in the headlong spurt to build.

Although there are two soft drink bottling plants near Sana'a and a textile mill in the city with over 1,500 employees, most industry is centered around the building trade and is carried out in small shop front establishments. Along the ring road (intended to encircle the city but now well within its limits) craftsmen produce stained glass windows, colorful iron doors, and wooden and aluminum window frames. Northeast of Bab Shu'ub are the brickyards and kilns that supply Sana'ani builders, and the stone-chipper's chisel is heard from early morning until twilight.

Furnished with woven straw cots and waterpipes, the communal rooms of hostels offer refuge to travelers.

The past merges conspicuously with the present in the streets of the western sector.

Until some years ago cars were a luxury, but today they are commonplace. There are new car showrooms, tire repair shops, automotive garages and gas stations scattered all over the city.

The water table beneath the Sana'ani plateau has dropped considerably in recent years, and the animal-drawn wells which previously furnished the city with water have mostly gone dry. The cries of the camel boys, the creaking of the wooden pulleys, and the measured hoofbeats on the wooden ramps are heard no more. Today two-thirds of Sana'a's water is supplied by a government-administered system of deep wells and mainlines north of the city. The rest is piped in from privately-owned wells on the outskirts of the capital.

There was no electricity in Sana'a until 1960 and as late as 1972 some bills were still computed by the number of bulbs burned out. Every business and nearly every house in the city has electricity now, and installation of underground power cables has already begun. Sana'a's electricity supply will soon be increased by a steam generating plant in al-Hudaidah.

Life continues essentially unchanged from centuries ago in the narrow lanes of the old Jewish quarter in Bir al-'Azab.

Until recent years, religious schools provided the only formal education and Sana'ani children who attended them studied Islam and the Koran, Arabic and elementary arithmetic. One secondary school in the city trained judges, teachers and government clerks. Today a system of public education goes through university level. Nearly all the old schools have been replaced by modern buildings with qualified Yemeni and expatriate teachers. Most schools offer both a morning and an afternoon session to accommodate all students. In addition, Sana'a has several technical and vocational schools and the only university in Yemen, with nearly 4,000 students and seven Faculties.

The entrance to Jamal Jameel, the oldest secondary school in the city. The plaques above the windows are inscribed with the Muslim profession of faith: "There is only one Allah and Muhammad is his Prophet."

In 1970 Sana'a opened the first university in Yemen, which now has seven Faculties and over 4,000 students.

Novel designs accent the windows of buildings in a new extension of Sana'a University located on Wadi Dahr Road.

This young businesswoman exemplifies the increasing number of Sana'ani women who are attaining higher levels of education and/or seeking jobs and careers outside the home.

Above: A woman employee of the Yemen Bank for Reconstruction and Development.

Below: These women are inspecting bottles in a soft drink plant on the outskirts of the city.

In 1979 luxury hotels began springing up in and around the city, offering international cuisine, swimming and tennis, and modern services.

There are four hospitals in the city, all with laboratories, x-ray equipment and operating rooms. The central laboratory has a modern parasitology unit and testing equipment for water purification, and there are several clinics and private x-ray concerns in the city.

Sana'a's international telecommunications services are via a satellite earth station located in al-Jiraf, north of the city. The earth station provides the capital with telephone, telex and telegram facilities to hundreds of countries. An automatic internal telephone system links the capital to all parts of the country.

Yemen's television station, located in Sana'a, produces news in Arabic and English, plays and variety productions, all in color, and there are both short and medium wave radio broadcasting stations in the city.

From the capital, Yemen's television station has broadcast local and foreign productions since 1975 with recent expanded color coverage to all parts of the country.

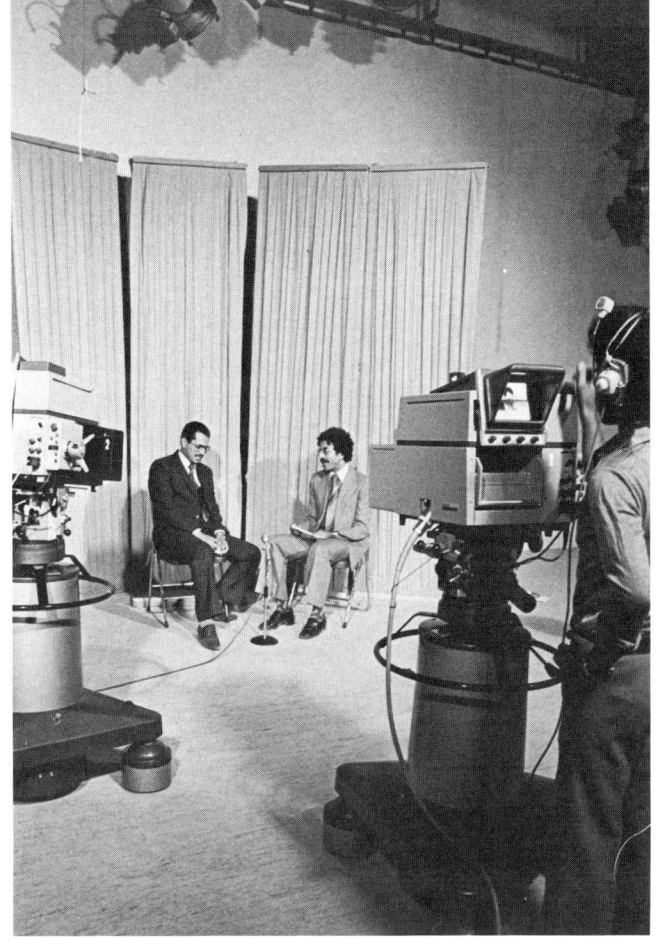

The Bank of Yemen towers over neighboring banks. The city has over twenty banking institutions serving its 200,000 residents.

Motorcycles which are used as taxis are decorated to catch the attention of prospective customers.

The city is linked to the airport twenty kilometers to the north by a divided highway.

Sana'a's international airport has modern passenger and baggage facilities and communications equipment. The national airline, Yemenia, has a fleet of four Boeing 727-200's which fly to many Middle Eastern cities, and other international airlines fly into the capital weekly.

Sana'a's international airport.

Dar al-Hajar (Rock Palace) is on the banks of Wadi Dahr fourteen kilometers northwest of the city. Cliffs rise nearly two hundred meters over the wide valley where apricot trees bloom in February.

Twelve kilometers from Sana'a the airport road passes the resort village of Rawdah, famed for its grape vineyards and ancient mosque. The Rawdah Palace is now a first-class hotel.

In 1962, the first asphalt road was completed in the Yemen Arab Republic, and today Sana'a is the central hub in a network of paved highways to Marib, al-Hudaidah, Ta'iz and Sa'dah. The capital is linked to the airport, twenty kilometers to the north, by a divided highway.

There are many scenic areas in the picturesque villages and countryside surrounding Sana'a. Impressive mosques and palaces, Turkish forts, and breathtaking mountain views entice the visitor away from the city.

Above: The capital's perimeter is continually expanding outward.

Below: The round towers and mudbrick dwellings of rural districts are falling into ruin, soon to disappear as modernization overtakes the western sector.

Hafidah

Hafidah, a beautiful, sad-eyed widow of twenty-nine, lives with her children in a small mudbrick house in a suburban quarter of Sana'a. Hafidah's husband, a poor man, died a year ago, leaving no money for his family, and her parents, who are very old, are not well-off enough to help their daughter.

However, taking care of herself and her children is nothing new for Hafidah, who has for years been earning her own way. She recently invested all her capital in a small shop on the first floor of her home, where she earns between one and two hundred *riyal*s a day selling canned food, soft drinks, toys and sweets.

Hafidah saved a long time to stock her shelves, and the day she opened for business was a proud one. She is well-known in the neighborhood, and everyone came to admire her supplies and buy a few items.

After only a few days, however, the women in the community, all of whom Hafidah regarded as her close friends, began to harass her. They reminded her that women are not supposed to own businesses or sell items that they have not made themselves. They disparage her because most of her customers are men and they say that, by running a shop, she is indecently encouraging male company.

The *shaikh* of the quarter has defended her. "You must remember that Hafidah has no husband or family who can support her," he chides them. "These days, it is not wrong for a woman to earn her living by running a respectable shop. Shame upon all of you for maligning a woman who has been your friend when you were sick or in trouble!"

Nevertheless, Hafidah is very worried about her reputation in the neighborhood and says she must close her shop if the women continue their unpleasantness toward her.

Hafidah was married at the age of ten to a thirty-year-old man. He paid a high dowry for her and, though he beat and abused her, it was a year before she could convince her father to allow her to return home. A second marriage was arranged by her family when she was twelve and her first child was born when she was thirteen. Her second husband was a good, patient man, but both he and their son became ill and died after only a year.

Hafidah's third husband took her as his second wife, and their marriage, though it lasted until his death, was riddled with periods of unhappiness and separation. This husband loved Hafidah, but was too afraid of his parents-in-law to divorce his first wife. Therefore, he divided his time between two households, with never enough money for either.

When her husband left her the first time, Hafidah was beside herself. In desperation, she tried to earn money by cleaning and taking in washing. As the months passed, she became more skilled, and her services included making dresses to order, painting ladies' hands and feet with *henna* and *naqsh*, and baking bread and cakes for the wealthier women in the quarter. By working hard and saving all she could, Hafidah was able to open her shop.

Hafidah is adamant that, although she has been successful as the family's breadwinner, it is not a life she would choose for her daughters. She feels unfortunate that circumstances have forced her to earn her own living, and believes that the practise of secluding women in the home, confining them to the role of wife and mother, is sound.

Hafidah declares, however, that she will never marry again. If a Sana'ani widow remarries, her deceased husband's family can claim his children, and she does not want to risk that happening to her. "Anyway," she says, "three failures are enough. Why should I take another chance and give up my independence just when life is becoming easier? If I must close my shop, I shall go back to earning a living by sewing and baking."

Reflections of a
Pattern of Living....

Yemen is famous for its architecture, and the houses of Sana'a are imposing monuments to the city's unique expression of the traditional Yemeni design. In addition, they are reflections of a lifestyle which endures from past centuries.

Sana'a is experiencing a building boom and the stone-chipper's chisel is heard from dawn to sunset. Blocks are painstakingly shaped, as they have been for centuries, . . .

... to form the stone foundations of new buildings.

The design of new minarets still incorporates the brickwork patterns which distinguish Sana'ani architecture.

Geometric patterns are carved in plaster to make the fanlights of Sana'a's famous windows.

The more elaborate windows have a plate of
open tracery on the outside. This is mounted
over an interior layer of a different design inset
with colored glass.

From stone foundations to terraced rooftops the walls of
Sana'ani houses rise as high as nine stories.

From stone foundations, the cliff-like walls of these baked brick houses rise five to nine stories. Near the top, the symmetry of the dwelling is broken by flat multi-level roofs, creating the terraces for which the city is famous. A thick, cohesive whitewash, made from an unusual limestone found near Sana'a, is used lavishly to accent brickwork border patterns, outline arches and arabesques around windows, and decorate the latticed window boxes staggered on the entrance wall. Sometimes an invocation to Allah is in whitewash script across the front of the house or worked into the tracery of a window.

Brickwork border patterns are featured on many façades.

A thick whitewash made from a special limestone found near Sana'a gives a 'gingerbread' effect.

False windows created by whitewashed arches and diamond patterns are added for symmetry and decoration. Here, workmen whitewash geometric brickwork borders . . .

. . . and whiten an entire wall.

Carved wooden window seats project from the walls of some homes and palaces.

False windows are added for uniformity and decoration, and thin circles of alabaster, mined near the city, are mounted in upright pairs across the façades. The rectangular glazed windows are topped by plaster fanlights, cut in geometric designs and inlaid with pieces of alabaster or, since the early years of this century, with brightly-colored glass. The really fine fanlights have a second plate of plaster tracery outside the colored layer, cut in a different design and either inset with clear glass or left open. These cathedral window-crowns shine like giant kaleidoscopes at night and cast jeweled patterns into the whitewashed rooms by day.

On the northern walls of houses are latticed brick, stone or wooden window boxes where perishable foods are kept cool. (Inscription on house: "This is from the grace of Allah.")

An invocation to Allah is worked into the tracery of many windows. The script in this window reads: "In the name of Allah the beneficent and merciful."

Circular alabaster windows or fanlights add a soft, diffuse light to the interior of the house.

The door from the street often opens into an inner courtyard. Ceilings are constructed of tree beams overlaid with smaller branches and, unlike this one, usually covered with plaster.

The entrance to the house from the street is into an inner courtyard, or directly into an area of small dark storage rooms, some of which were formerly used for stables. Waist-high bins of wheat, sugar, corn and rock salt, with a grinding mill, are kept in these rooms.

The water table has dropped below the level of many old wells and cisterns, and most of Sana'a's water now comes through a network of mainlines from wells outside the capital.

There are stacks of cardboard and firewood for the earthenware oven, and a well, which once supplied the household with water, now stands idle.

Some households rely on commercial delivery for their entire water supply.

Some doors are beautifully carved...

The wide stone staircase which winds up through the house to the roof has steep, uneven risers and numerous landings. Doors open from the staircase into lobbies at each upper level.

. . . with great metal knockers. . .

. . . and large wooden locks. . .

. . . secured with enormous keys.

In addition to the wooden locks some houses are further secured by Yemeni padlocks.

In the traditional kitchen the stove is a masonry block inset with vertical earthenware ovens (*tannurs*). The sink is supplied by water stored in a twenty-liter aluminum can.

Above the storage area are the living and sleeping rooms where the family eats, entertains relatives or close friends, and sleeps. The kitchen may also be on this level, where the women in the household share in the preparation of family meals.

The kitchen is a dark, poorly-ventilated room which becomes intolerably hot and smoky when the fires are lit. Its walls are blackened by soot and if there are windows they are small and tightly-shuttered to keep out dust and drafts. Usually the smoke escapes through small outlets on the northern wall or is conveyed through the wall to chimneys on the roof.

Charcoal braziers supplement the *tannu*rs.

There is little or no counter space, for Sana'ani women prepare food in pots and on trays while kneeling or squatting on the floor. The sink is in a waist-high masonry block with a channel for water to drain to the outside. There may be running water in the kitchen with faucets over the sink, or water may be carried in to be stored in twenty-liter aluminum cans or earthenware jars. The stove is also a masonry block with vertical pits for the cylindrical clay oven used for baking and, when covered by a grate, for grilling and boiling. Charcoal, wood and sometimes dung are used as fuel in this *tannur*. A charcoal brazier supplements the *tannur*, and nowadays many women also have small gas stoves with ovens.

*Tannur*s, **the earthenware ovens used in traditional kitchens, are made in the city.**

There is little counter space and women prepare food in pots and on trays while kneeling or squatting on the floor.

The kitchen has recessed shelves over the sink and stove where aluminum saucepans, stone pots and flat bread baskets are stored. There are tin cans for saving left-over bits of charcoal, wooden sticks and spoons for stirring food and poking the fire, and long-necked clay jugs for steeping *qishr* and incensed water. Leeks, potatoes and fresh basil hang in baskets on the wall. Though the stone *mazhagah* is used for grinding spices, herbs and grains, many families own an electric blender, and some also have a pressure cooker and an electric teakettle.

The *shubbak*, a cupboard with wooden doors recessed in the wall near the kitchen, serves as a refrigerator. An earthenware jar of water kept in the *shubbak* is cooled by the wind blowing through the perforated brickwork on the *shubbak*'s exterior wall, and the evaporation from the jar keeps perishable food stored in the cupboard fresh for days. Holes in the bottom of the *shubbak* allow women to peer down to the street without being seen.

Evaporation from a large earthenware jar filled with drinking water keeps food stored in the *shubbak* cool and fresh.

Bathrooms are a functional arrangement of raised stones over a 'long drop' latrine. Urine is channeled into a vertical drainage surface on the outside wall of the building where, in Sana'a's low humidity, it dries quickly. Some houses have installed pipes over the drainage surface which lead to underground sumps. Solid waste falls through a masonry shaft into a chamber at street level. Once dry, it is collected and used as fuel in the public baths, and the resulting ash fertilizes the market gardens. To wash, one sits or squats on raised stones in front of a stone cylinder which supports a basin of water. As in the kitchen, there may be running water in bathrooms, but water is still often stored in earthenware jars.

The functional arrangement of raised stones for washing has been retained in this renovated bathroom.

The *mafraj* is usually a long room with wide shuttered windows built low to provide views of the landscape from cushions on the floor.

A typical *mafraj* with alabaster fanlights, plastered ceiling beams, and walls and shelves decorated with plaster motifs and calligraphy.

The highest level of the house, where the air is clearest and the views most scenic, is reserved for the *mafraj,* the center of Sana'ani social life. The *mafraj* is usually a long room with wide shuttered windows on all but the northern wall (to prevent smoke entering from the kitchen outlets). These windows, framed in plaster motifs and calligraphy, are built low to provide views of the landscape and city from mattresses on the floor. Alabaster or stained glass fanlights illuminate the room and small rectangular openings beside the windows provide ventilation. On every wall are small plaster shelves, also decorated by relief floral designs or quotations from the Koran, and recessed cupboards with colored glass doors. The plastered ceiling is supported by unhewn walnut branches covered by a thick layer of palm leaves, bushes and twigs.

The furnishings in Sana'ani homes are simple and multi-purpose, since everything from socializing to eating is done sitting on the floor. All rooms have a continuous arrangement of colorful mattresses against the walls with bolsters for back and arm rests. The floors are carpeted and brass trays serve as coffee tables. Before the introduction of electric light bulbs and fluorescent lamps, rooms were lit by burning sesame oil in copper lanterns or in stone or alabaster bowls.

The *mafraj* contains the most beautiful of the family's furnishings, and its walls are hung with rich tapestries, ornamental *jambiyah*s, brocade purses containing the Koran, and solemn pictures of *imam*s, presidents and family patriarchs. There are waterpipes, their brightly-colored coiled hoses enrobed in hand-crocheted covers, and tobacco and incense are stored in ornate silver boxes and burned in earthenware braziers. Graceful brass containers with doily lids serve as spittoons for *qat,* and some families have magnificent brass and silver candle stands.

The houses that are being built today in the western sector and on the outskirts of the city are of modern Arab style: one- or two-story structures surrounded by walled gardens. The rooms for living and sleeping open off a spacious central area, and the large windows are protected by bars. There are no stables or storerooms, and the *tannur*s and *shubbak*s are replaced by gas stoves and refrigerators. With the influx of foreigners, living styles are changing, and so is the architectural design of the city's houses. However, most Sana'anis, young and old, cling to the conventional family home, a manifestation of the invariable serenity of daily Yemeni life.

The *mafraj* is spread with carpets and furnished with colorful mattresses, bolsters and arm rests. Large brass trays on the floor serve as tables for waterpipes, ewers and incense burners.

Lutfiyah

Lutfiyah is an attractive, vivacious woman in her late thirties. She runs an extended household in the Old Town, which consists of her husband, six of their children, two of their sons' wives and one grandchild. Lutfiyah's *tabinah*, her husband's first wife, lives in an upstairs apartment with her son and daughter-in-law.

Lutfiyah's husband, who owns a profitable antique shop in the *suq*, is over sixty and would like to marry off his four daughters before he gets too old. He has had several proposals from men who are already married, but Lutfiyah has protested so vehemently that he has had to turn them all down. She vows that her beautiful girls will never be any man's second wife.

Lutfiyah's husband was married to his first wife for many years before deciding on a second marriage. He was, in fact, quite content with his first wife, but she grew tired of his demands and pushed him to find a second, younger spouse. He arranged with Lutfiyah's father to marry her when she was only ten. Lutfiyah's mother was so stricken by this that she became critically ill, and the father agreed to wait until the girl reached puberty before allowing her to leave their home. However, when her mother died a year later, Lutfiyah joined her husband's household.

Her *tabinah* treated Lutfiyah like a servant. She did less and less work herself and expected the girl to cook, clean and wait on her and her guests. When Lutfiyah complained, the woman threatened to tell their husband that she had caught the girl at the window unveiled. Terrified at what he would do if he thought this were true, Lutfiyah thenceforth obeyed and kept silent.

When she reached puberty, Lutfiyah immediately became pregnant, and her first baby was born when she was fourteen. Her husband was elated and moved the family into a house in the Old Town which Lutfiyah had chosen. He also showered his young wife with gold and new dresses, and the older *tabinah* became jealous. She did everything she could to insult and humiliate the girl, but the husband remained enthralled, and his first wife took to returning more and more frequently to her father's house. As Lutfiyah's other children were born, she replaced her husband's first wife in his affections and became the principal woman in his household.

Today Lutfiyah and her *tabinah* live under the same roof in relative peace and mutual tolerance. Occasionally, the older woman joins Lutfiyah and her girls for morning tea but, for the most part, she leads her own life in her upper floor apartment. Lutfiyah spends her days in the company of her daughters and daughters-in-law, who describe her as a kind, hard-working mother who treats them all equally well.

Lutfiyah blames the difficulties and unhappiness of her young married life on having a *tabinah,* and she thinks the position of a second wife in a household is intolerable. She knows, too, that a girl's mother-in-law can also make life miserable and is determined that her daughters will marry into households of gracious, amiable women who will treat them well.

"Though I love my husband and respect his wishes on many matters, I intend to stand firm for my girls. No *tabinah*s, no cruel mothers-in-law. I want them to have a better life than I have had." Then, never serious for very long, Lutfiyah adds, "My husband is too old and weak now to beat me, so if he gets angry, who cares?"

... That Has Endured For Centuries

Changes in Sana'ani patterns of living have occurred in the last two decades, resulting from expatriates coming into the city and from the exposure of young men and women, both through travel and television, to life in other countries. The older generation admits that customs and mores, especially those involving the role of women, are now changing so rapidly that the lives of their sons and daughters will scarcely resemble their own. However, for the present the city's Muslim residents cling to established proprieties and routines, not wishing to trade their leisurely lifestyle for the feverish pace of western living.

The patriarchal family is the foundation of Sana'ani society, and several generations usually live together in an extended household.

The patriarchal family is the foundation of Sana'ani society, and no one lives alone. When a man marries, his wife leaves her family to join the hierarchy of his household. Though Muslim law permits men to have as many as four wives, today only a few older Sana'ani men have more than one. However, young marriages and a high divorce rate make it likely that most people, men and women, will have more than one spouse in the course of their lives.

The extended household consists, then, of a man, his wife or wives, his unmarried children, and his married sons and their wives and children. It may also include other relatives, such as a widowed or divorced mother or sister.

The responsibilities of adulthood come early and, around the age of ten, girls begin to veil and don the *sharshaf*, the black outer garment of Sana'ani women.

The men in the family are the wage-earners, working from Saturday to Thursday in shops, industries or government offices. They manage all household affairs that require contact with the outside world, and do most of the shopping, including buying clothes for their wives and children. Men pray together in the mosques and socialize with one another at work and during afternoon *qat* sessions. The Sana'ani man is acquainted only with the women of his immediate family and may never have seen the wife of his best friend. His own wife was chosen for him by his parents, and he saw her face for the first time on the night of his wedding.

Children play in the side streets and empty lots of their neighborhoods.

Keeping house includes shaking the city's heavy
dust out of rugs and blankets, . . .

. . . washing clothes, . . .

... and spreading them on the roof to dry.

Sana'ani women are supported by their fathers if unmarried or divorced, or by their husbands or his family if married or widowed. The honor of the family, a prime social evaluation in Sana'a, rests on the woman, and she is encouraged to remain at home and avoid the company of men whenever possible. When she does go out for visiting, occasional shopping, or trips to the *hammam,* she wears a veil, which is synonymous with high morals and sophisticated city life. Even indoors, she usually wears the *lithmah,* which she wraps around her head in such a way that it can quickly be pulled up to cover all of her face except the eyes. The wealthier and higher ranking a family is, the more secluded are its women.

Spinning goat hair into yarn for carpets.

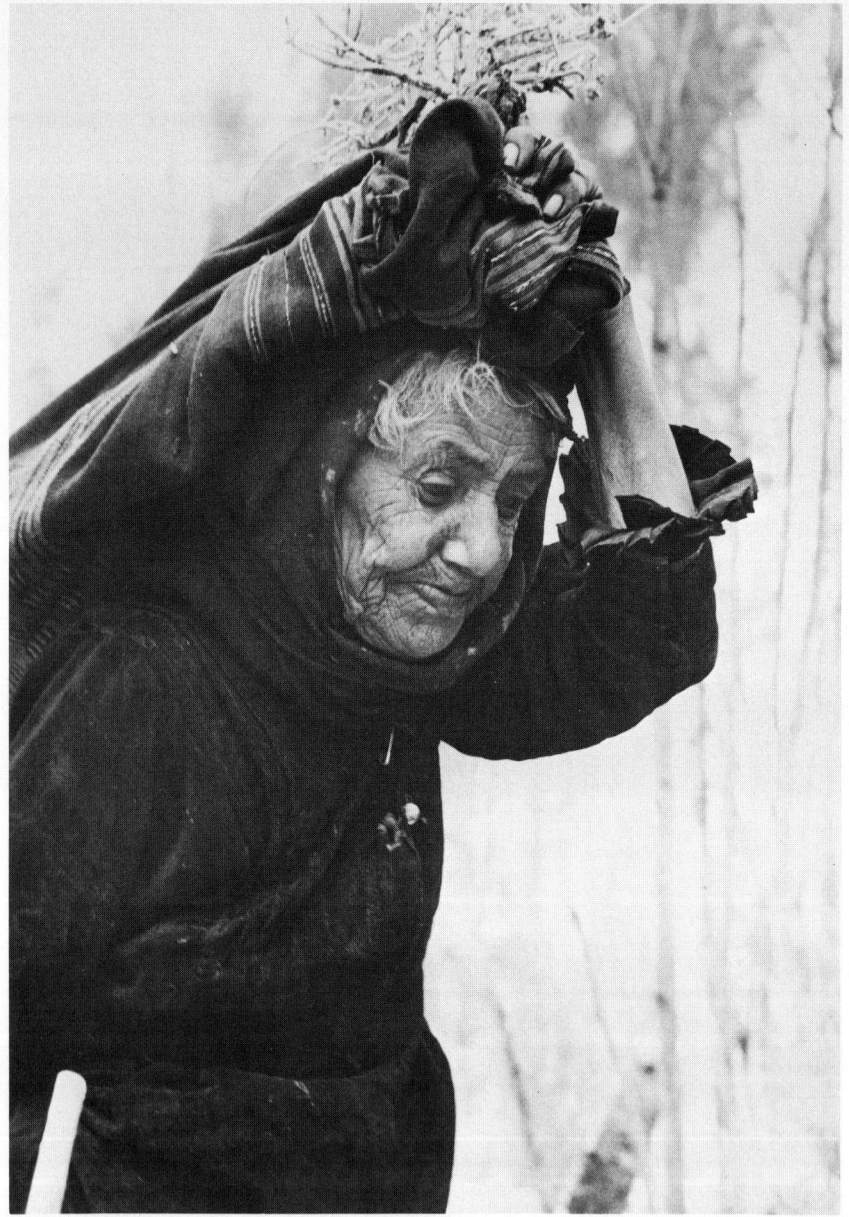
Gathering fuel for the earthenware oven.

Women value a supportive husband, a close family and the accumulation of personal wealth, usually gold jewelry and dresses. They admire other women for their beauty, their polite and modest behavior, and how they rear their children. Their role is to cook and clean and to take care of their offspring, and life is an unvaried, ordered progression through childhood, puberty, marriage and motherhood.

Like their men, Sana'ani women spend their waking hours in the company of members of their own sex. Unlike men, however, women do have occasion to serve food or drink to male gatherings. At such times, under the protection of the veil, they learn much about the men in their social circle. It is a rare bride who has not seen her groom's face or heard his voice before their wedding night.

Babies are welcome additions to Sana'ani families, regarded as gifts from Allah and assuring their mother of a preferred status in the household. Although there is a customary preference for sons, parents appreciate both sexes for differently-timed joys and benefits. Girls help with cleaning and cooking while they are growing up and increase the family wealth through dowries when they are married. Boys bring home strong young wives to help their mothers with the housework and can be counted on for the financial support of aged parents.

Children are raised in a loving, permissive atmosphere, playing, eating and sleeping at will. Adults welcome them to their gatherings but don't worry about them when they choose to be elsewhere. By the age of six, they may go to school and begin to help with household chores. Girls learn to clean and cook, attend afternoon *tafritah* with their mothers and, at ten, begin to wear the veil. Though education is not as important for girls as for boys, girls may, if they enjoy it and do well, go to school until they marry, usually at thirteen or fourteen. Boys attend school, helping in the afternoons in their father's shop or even attending business meetings and *qat* sessions with him. They, too, assume the responsibilities of an adult at an early age, and it is not uncommon to see boys of twelve selling, driving cars or serving as soldiers. Sometime around the age of fifteen, a boy is given a *jambiyah* by his father and begins to wear a *mashaddah*. He may be married at seventeen or eighteen.

The individual concentration with which westerners attack their work is inconceivable to Sana'anis, and "tomorrow, Allah willing" is an oft-repeated phrase. All chores are carried out in a relaxed, leisurely fashion, ideally in the congenial company of others. Time is of little importance, and the only public clock, a gift to the city from West Germany, chimes the quarter hours unheeded.

The day is structured by the five calls to prayer, and dawn is heralded by the voice of the *mu'adhdhin* amplified over the sleeping city. The pious rise, wash their faces, hands and feet, and cover themselves with clean clothes. Facing Mecca, they recite verses and phrases from the Koran, which they accompany by prescribed postures of sitting, standing, bowing and prostration. Though women pray at home, most Muslim men go to the mosque at least once a day.

Dough is stretched over a pillow form (*makhbazah*) to shape the flat circles of pocket bread.

After prayer, a light breakfast of bread and tea may be taken, though many prefer to wait until eight o'clock for a substantial meal of liver, eggs, beans or porridge.

While the men are at work, the women care for the children and clean the house—airing blankets, shaking the city's heavy dust out of cushions and mattresses, and sweeping and mopping the floors. Older girls may be in charge of washing clothes in large flat pans and hanging them to dry on the roof. Often friends, draped in the *sitarah,* drop by to drink a glass of *qishr,* gossip, or extend an invitation for *tafritah.*

Around eleven o'clock the women of the household begin preparations for lunch, the most important meal of the day. They set the bread dough to rise, fire up the *tannur* with bits of wood and charcoal, and perhaps kill and pluck a fresh chicken.

The *makhbazah* is used to thrust the dough against the vertical oven wall where it clings and bakes in a few minutes.

The day is structured by the five calls to prayer when the voice of the *mu'adhdhin* is amplified over the city from the numerous mosques.

Bab al-Yemen is the only gate still standing of the original five into the Old Town.

The *suq,* or market, begins just inside
Bab al-Yemen.

Locally-made earthenware vessels are sold in the *suq*.

Selling herbs and spices for Sana'ani cuisine, which is enhanced by such distinctive flavors as cumin, fenugreek, garlic, cardamom and red pepper.

Live chickens are brought to market in tear-shaped straw baskets.

Many imported items are for sale in the *suq*, including colorful Asian fabric and hand-painted Indian trunks.

Selling the carpets and cushions that furnish *mafraj*es.

In Sana'ani homes the most decorative *mafraj* **is the center of male social activity.**

Three varieties of windows are found in a *mafraj:* the wide glazed windows offer views of the city, the colorful fanlights illuminate the room, and the small rectangular openings beside the fanlights provide ventilation.

When guests join the family for meals, men and women dine in separate rooms.

Hilbah, **Yemen's national dish,** is a whipped fenugreek dip served in stone vessels. Most Sana'anis eat it every day for they believe that, without *hilbah* to soften and line the stomach, the afternoon's *qat* could not be enjoyed.

A variety of breads, stews and vegetable dishes are spread on colorful plastic sheets on the floor of the *mafraj.*

Qat is one of the major crops grown in the fertile fields surrounding Sana'a.

Above: In the afternoon men take their daily supply of *qat* to a friend's *mafraj* to relax, socialize and discuss business, remaining until the evening call to prayer.

Below: As the mouthpiece of the *mada'ah* is passed from guest to guest, the long hoses coil through *qat* leaves strewn on the floor of the *mafraj*.

The stained glass windows of Sana'a are works of art...

. . . shining in the night like giant kaleidoscopes.

A carved wooden window seat adorns the wall of this Sana'ani building.

The Yemeni cuisine is a simple, healthy diet based on unrefined cereals and grains. Round, flat loaves of bread, baked daily from sorghum, barley and wheat flours, are eaten with every meal. Milk, meat and vegetable dishes are also appreciated, and Sana'anis, who generally frown on imported canned or frozen foods, pay exorbitant prices for fresh meat and vegetables grown nearby. The recipes from these local foods have been passed down from mother to daughter through many generations, but are today prepared with an odd combination of modern and conventional equipment.

As flames spring from the *tannur,* singeing the already-blackened wall, the kitchen fills with smoke. The women take turns stepping outside for fresh air, and the cooking is accomplished in seeming disorganization. Chicken, flavored with cumin or thyme, browns in a clay pot on a charcoal brazier, and meat broth simmers in a pressure cooker on a gas stove. Using their fingers or a wooden spoon, the women beat *hilbah,* a dip made by soaking fenugreek seeds in water and whipping them to a yellow froth. *Zahawiq,* a spicy sauce of tomatoes, garlic, mint and red pepper is made in a blender or ground by hand on a grindstone, and *khubz* is baked by stretching the dough across the *makhbazah* and thrusting it against the sides of the red-hot *tannur,* thus insuring that the women's forearms remain free of unfeminine hair. Peelings, cores and leaves are thrown out the window or onto the floor, to be swept up by one of the younger girls with a straw hand broom.

Grindstones are common utensils in Sana'ani kitchens. This *mazhagah* is being used to make *zahawiq*, a spicy blend of tomatoes, garlic, cumin and red peppers.

The men return about one-thirty and, if there are no guests, the family takes the midday meal together. Sana'ani generosity, however, usually insures that friends, or even complete strangers, are taken in to share a meal. In this case, the women eat separately, often in the kitchen.

The food is served in metal pots, stone vessels and china bowls placed on aluminum trays on the floor. Round circles of freshly-baked *khubz* and *maluj* are on flat baskets. Though plates, knives and forks are not common, spoons are used to add sauces and vegetables to serving dishes of rice and salad. Everyone, using only his right hand, eats by dipping torn pieces of bread into the communal pots and bowls.

The meal may begin with white radishes dipped in a fenugreek vinegar sauce. These may be followed by wheat or sorghum porridge served with honey and ghee, or *shafut,* a maize pancake soaked in sour milk and spiced with mint or thyme. There may be *bint al-sahn,* a honeyed yeast bread, or *susi,* a bread, eggs and butter casserole, and there are usually potatoes, peppers, beans or okra, and a meat or chicken stew. Always there is *hilbah,* mixed with herbs and spices and served with meat broth in a stone vessel. Sana'anis believe that, without *hilbah* to line and soften the stomach, the afternoon's *qat* could not be enjoyed. Water is the only beverage served with meals, but, after a light dessert of custard flavored with cinnamon, cloves and cardamom, the family goes to another room to drink tea or *qishr,* and perhaps to smoke the waterpipe or nibble sweets.

Around three o'clock the men and women of the family set off in different directions to join a neighborhood gathering, some carrying *qat* wrapped in colored plastic. There are always several parties to choose from, often those of weddings, births and even funerals, and, invited or not, everyone is welcome. Those who don't chew *qat* or smoke the waterpipe come to relax, be with friends or, in the case of men, discuss business.

Meals are eaten by dipping torn pieces of freshly-baked bread into communal pots.

Leaving her shoes and veil at the entrance to the *mafraj,* the guest at *tafritah* circles among those already present, bending to kiss hands and faces in greeting. Then she chooses her own place, sitting with one leg bent under her, the other knee upraised so as not to impolitely expose the soles of her feet. There is room for everyone, shoulder-to-shoulder on the floor cushions or, in the case of children who accompany their mothers, perched on the wide windowsills.

For *tafritah* many women make up their faces, wear their best clothes and jewelry, and paint their hands and feet with *henna.* Married women wear a head scarf and a wide brocade headband. Soon the room is lit by a hundred colors, and gold and silver shimmer from the folds of brocade, silk and filmy nylon. Here at last are the unseen faces of Sana'ani women, all the more captivating because they are seen by so few.

The hostess circulates glasses of hot sweet tea or spicy *qishr,* and bowls of raisins, popcorn, nuts and roasted lentils. A few of the women begin to smoke the *mada'ah* and chew *qat,* tossing choice sprigs to nearby friends and guests. The scents of thirty perfumes mingle with the pungency of incense and tobacco, and the long hoses of the waterpipes coil through discarded *qat* leaves strewn on the floor. The atmosphere is relaxed and pleasant as the women talk about their families or their health and gossip and joke with one another. Sometimes an older woman will tell a story or enact a skit. There is usually music from a cassette recorder and, from time to time, two guests join hands and perform the traditional Sana'ani dance, feet moving in formal patterns, knees and shoulders swaying to the elusive Arabic rhythm.

The five precepts of Islam are profession of faith, prayer, almsgiving, fasting and pilgrimage.

The men are more serious about chewing *qat*. After only an hour, a layer of green leaves carpets the floor and cheeks reach an incredible degree of distension. As the men begin to feel the stimulating effects of the *qat*, their eyes become glazed and conversation is more animated. Often they compose or recite poetry, or discuss politics or current affairs. It has been said that more business is accomplished during the afternoon *qat* session than during the morning work hours.

On special occasions, guests at an afternoon gathering may listen or dance to the music of singers and musicians, many of whom still perform the Yemeni bedouin songs. The musicians may strum the lute or simply beat a rhythm on drums or metal trays.

Before sunset, the women reappear in the streets, veiled silhouettes hurrying homeward. The men attend the twilight prayer call, then return to work, visit cafes and shops, or play chess with friends. After the fifth and final call to prayer signals an end to the day's activities, they return home to join the women in front of the television set. Some families have a light meal of yoghurt, bread and fruit before retiring for the night.

The afternoon is spent in the company of others, chewing *qat* or smoking the *mada'ah*.

Hassan

Hassan is a Sana'ani businessman in his late twenties, educated in the United States and now living with his wife and small daughter in his father's household in the Old Town. Hassan spends his mornings attending board meetings, visiting project sites, and conducting telephone conferences with business colleagues abroad. In the afternoon he chews *qat*.

Qat is a bush of the coffee family which grows in the fields and on the mountain terraces of Yemen. Though only a mild, non-addictive stimulant, it is prized by Yemenis for its euphoria-producing qualities.

Qat has been grown in Yemen since the fifteenth century, when it was used to cure melancholy, inspire thinkers and instill warriors with greater physical prowess. Today its use is widespread, and afternoon *qat* sessions are a deeply-rooted, respectable social custom in Sana'a. The leaves are chewed every afternoon by shopkeepers, laborers, taxi drivers and government workers, either on the job or in *mafraj*es all over the city. As a source of entertainment, *qat* is the focal point of social gatherings, including weddings, celebrations and feasts and, very often, of political and business meetings as well. "*Qat* sessions," explains Hassan," are the Yemeni version of tea and cocktail parties found in other societies, except that they are much more stimulating."

The afternoon sessions Hassan attends are in his father's or a friend's *mafraj*. They are open to everyone, and guests bring their own *qat*. Hassan looks forward to these gatherings, which are forums of intellectual exchange on everything from local news to world politics. He insists that, without the mental stimulation and physical relaxation he obtains from them, he couldn't cope with the extra hours of reading reports and writing letters that he must do every evening.

To chew *qat*, one selects a handful of tender, shiny leaves, chews them lightly, and stores them in the cheek. The juice of the leaves is swallowed, but the pulp remains in the cheek all afternoon, distending it by a couple of inches. Water, often imbued with incense, or sweetened tea is sipped to offset the bitterness and astringency of the leaves. To be fully enjoyed, *qat* must be chewed in the company of others and only after a full meal that includes *hilbah*.

Individuals differ in their reactions to *qat*, but most claim that, after using it, they eat less, feel physically stronger, and are able to think and work more intensively and creatively. They insist, also, that the ascorbic acid in *qat* keeps them free of colds and flu.

Opponents of *qat* say it causes insomnia, intestinal disorders and a dangerous loss of appetite. Hassan laughs at these claims. "With the price of *qat* the way it is," he scoffs, "no one chews enough to suffer these ill effects."

As Yemen's most profitable cash crop, *qat* plays an important role in the nation's economy. Because it is marketed locally at such a high return, requires little care and is harvested throughout the year, more and more villages and regions are abandoning other crops to grow *qat* exclusively.

Government leaders worry about the negative effects the increasing cultivation of *qat* is having on export crops and food for local consumption, but Hassan and his supporters point out that small farmers cultivating *qat* make more money per acre than they could with any other crop, insuring a more even distribution of wealth. He says that the income of *qat* farmers, if channeled into real estate, trade or industry, can become a positive force in the country's economy. In any case, *qat* has become so institutionalized in Yemen that experts agree any effort to reduce its cultivation or curtail its use would surely result in failure.

In Keeping With Islam...

The pattern of Sana'ani days is varied by the Ramadan month of fasting, the pilgrimage to Mecca, and the feasts that are associated with these religious occasions.

On the first Friday of the eighth lunar month, Sana'anis celebrate 'Id Rajab in honor of the acceptance of Islam by Yemenis. Today, this holiday is associated with women; men and children spend the day visiting their female relatives. The visitors are served cakes, sweets and soft drinks, and sprinkled with perfume or cologne. When they leave, it is customary to give money to the women and children of the household.

Ramadan is the ninth month of the lunar Muslim year and is set aside as a time of fasting to commemorate Allah's revelations to the Prophet Muhammad. It is believed that during Ramadan the gates of hell are closed and the gates of paradise are open, and that the sins of those who keep the fast will be pardoned.

When the new moon is sighted, Muslims refrain from eating, drinking or smoking from dawn until sunset of each day. Everyone is required to fast except the sick, the weak, and small children. Soldiers on duty or travelers on long, necessary journeys may refrain from fasting but are required to make up any days missed.

The fast imposes a hardship on those who must continue their jobs, especially laborers, merchants and women who cook and care for small children. It is even more difficult when it occurs in the dryness of Sana'a's hot summer season. However, the suffering instills a feeling of closeness to Allah and communion with one's fellow man. Those who can spare the time go more often to the mosque, even between the calls to prayer, and read the Koran at work or at home. The city's poor and disabled are assured of sizable donations during Ramadan as almsgiving, an obligation of Islam, bestows a special grace on the benefactor at this holy time. Health and well-being during the fast are favorite topics of conversation, and friends part in wishing one another a blessed Ramadan.

For the devout Muslim the day is woven around the silent moments spent studying the Koran.

The pages of this handwritten Koran, which is several hundred years old, are decorated with intricate gold-leaf patterns.

During Ramadan the activities of day and night are completely altered, and the mornings are singularly quiet in the fasting city of Sana'a. The streets are empty except for a few children, and the shops and businesses stay closed until after the noon prayer.

As the afternoon shadows lengthen, the mosques are full of men awaiting the end of the day's abnegation. When the sun sets a cannon sounds, and everyone shares a breakfast of dates and bread before leaving the mosque to return home. Nights are a time of feasting, chewing *qat*, dancing and singing. Shops stay open until after midnight, and the television station features special programs, broadcasting until very late. The cannon sounds again to begin the fast at break of day.

'Id al-Fitr, or the Feast of Breaking the Fast, is celebrated the first three days of Shawwal, the month after Ramadan. After thirty days of fasting, it is a joyous time of prayer and feasts, and many marriages occur during 'Id al-Fitr. Sana'anis leave the city to return to hometowns or villages, or to visit relatives in other parts of the country, and city life doesn't usually return to normal until a week after Ramadan.

All Muslims who can afford it are expected at least once in their lives to make the pilgrimage to Mecca to worship at the *ka'bah* and spend one day at Mt. Arafat. Many also go to Medina for eight days to visit the tombs of Muhammad and the first caliphs, and to perform the rites of forty prayers. The *hajj*, which occurs during the twelfth month of the lunar year, brings great honor to the returning pilgrim and to his family, and one who has been to Mecca is respectfully referred to thereafter as *al-Hajj*.

The Feast of the Pilgrimage, 'Id al-Adha (or 'Id Arafat), begins on the tenth day of Dhu al-Hijjah, the month of the *hajj*, and lasts for four days. Sana'ani children in new dresses and suits parade with proud fathers, and each household serves special cakes to friends and relatives. Many families slaughter a sheep, commemorating Abraham's obedient willingness to sacrifice his son to Allah.

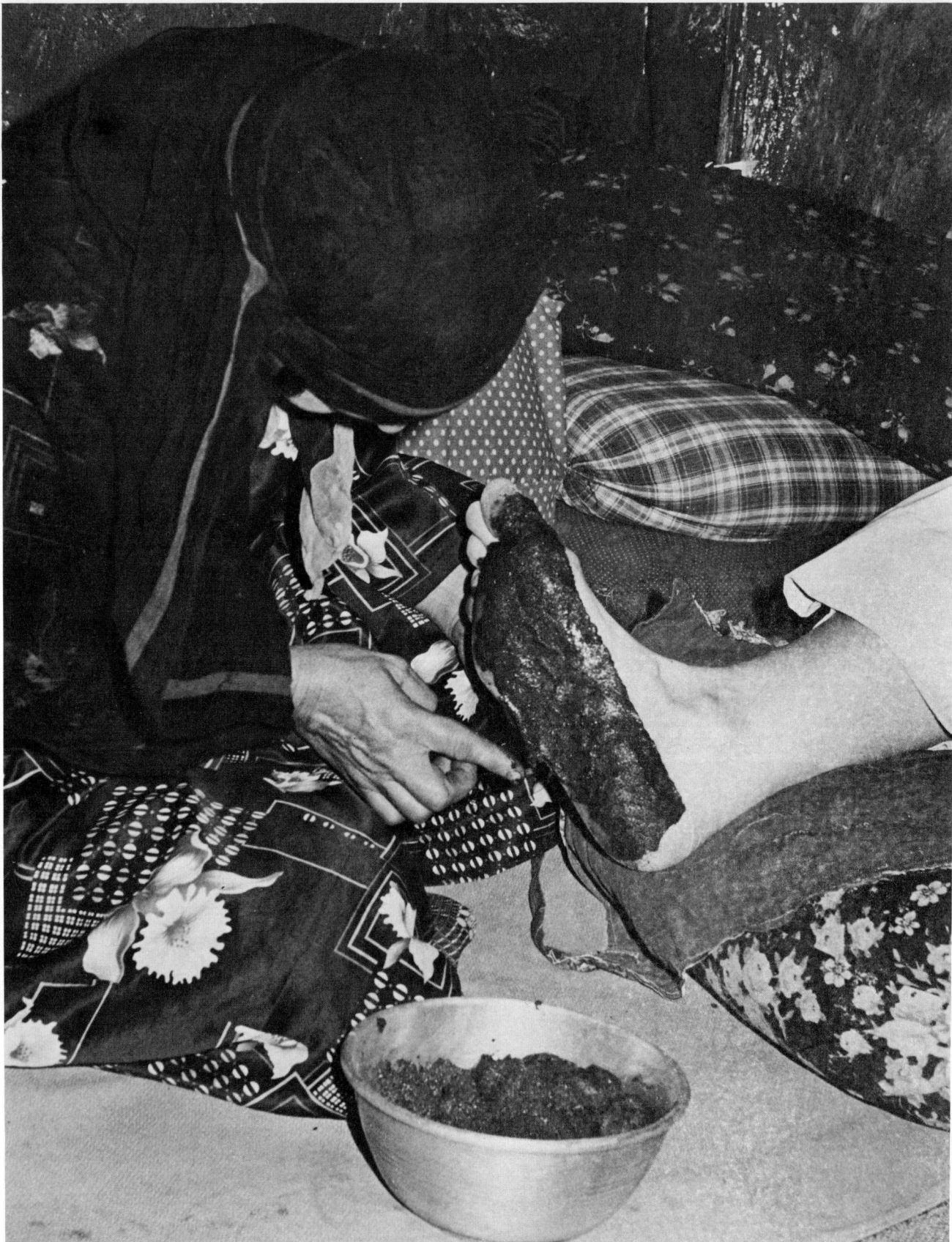

...And Its Social Conventions

Sana'anis are gregarious people, and the occasions of weddings, births and even deaths are marked by a series of social activities open to all. Though the men usually only participate in the events of the first few days, the celebration parties for women may continue for weeks.

The terms of marriages in Sana'a are stipulated by a civil contract between the families of the bride and groom. Parents, sometimes with the help of a professional match-maker, decide on spouses for their offspring, who generally must accept the choice. In order to keep inheritance within the social circle, many marriages are arranged between distant cousins or close friends of the family. However, the separation of the sexes from an early age insures that the couple do not know each other.

As childbearers and housekeepers, women are essential in the household and Sana'ani men pay a high dowry for their wives. The marriage contract specifies the amount of this bride-price, which has, in the past, been between 25,000 and 40,000 *riyal*s, but is now limited by law to 15,000. The bride's father uses this money for wedding festivities, for gifts for his daughter and her mother, and for savings. The bride receives a portion, the *mahr*, to buy gold, dresses and toiletries for her wedding. She may also put some of it aside as security in case of divorce.

Sana'ani women often have their hands and feet painted with *henna*. The roots and leaves of the *henna* plant, when ground, dissolved in water and mixed with oil, produce a reddish brown dye used since the beginning of civilization for cosmetic purposes.

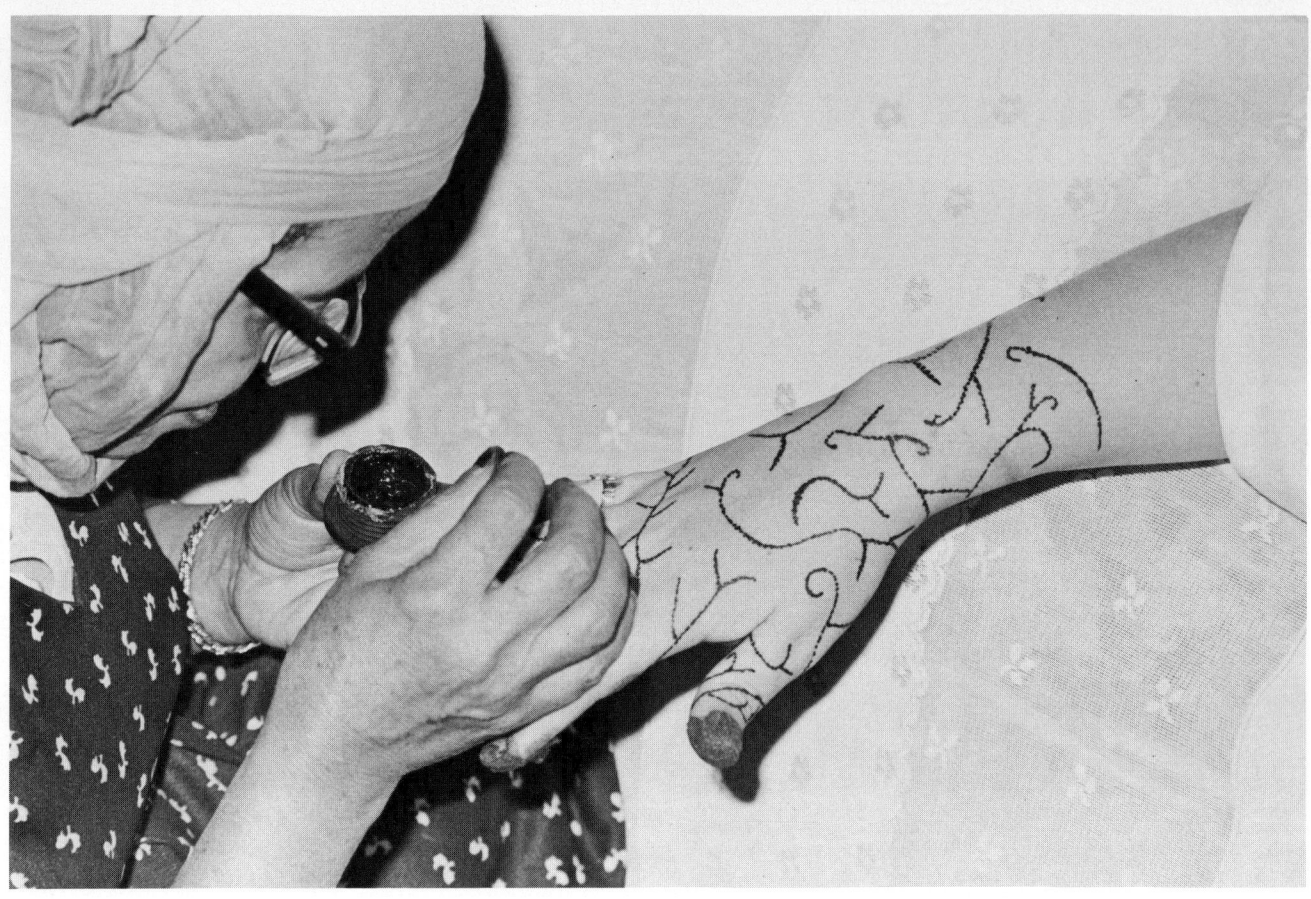

After the *henna* dries, vinelike patterns of *naqsh*, a black dye, are dotted on arms and hands to enhance beauty on special occasions.

Separate parties for the bride and groom begin a few days before the marriage and continue for at least a week thereafter. A day or two before the wedding, after the bridal party visits the *hammam*, a bridal attendant paints the hands and feet of the bride and her friends with *henna* and vine-like patterns of *naqsh*. The bride, completely covered by an embroidered cloth, is ceremoniously led into the room amidst the chanting and trilling of hired musicians and guests. On the wedding day the bride appears at the afternoon party in white gown and headdress, which can be the formal gold *taj*, inlaid with semi-precious stones and decorated with hanging pendants, or a tiara and white veil. In the evening she goes in *sharshaf* to join the household of her husband.

On the evening of the wedding the bride goes in *sharshaf* **to join the household of her husband.**

The groom, too, on the day of the wedding is surrounded by friends and hired musicians who accompany him to the mosque at twilight. After prayer, the procession wends its way homeward, chanting and carrying lighted candles and incense. In the streets beneath electric light bulbs strung up for the occasion, the men sing and dance with upraised *jambiyah*s, remaining with the groom until his bride arrives.

A luncheon party is held for the groom and his friends the day after the wedding, and for the bride and her friends on the third day. The bride returns to her family for three days of parties when she has been married one week.

All these social functions, hosted in turn by the families of the bride and groom, serve to strengthen new family ties and provide moral support for the couple, easing the trauma of marriage to a virtual stranger. The bride, particularly, is encouraged by the money, jewelry and finery she receives, and takes pride in them as statements of her honor, beauty and value in her new household.

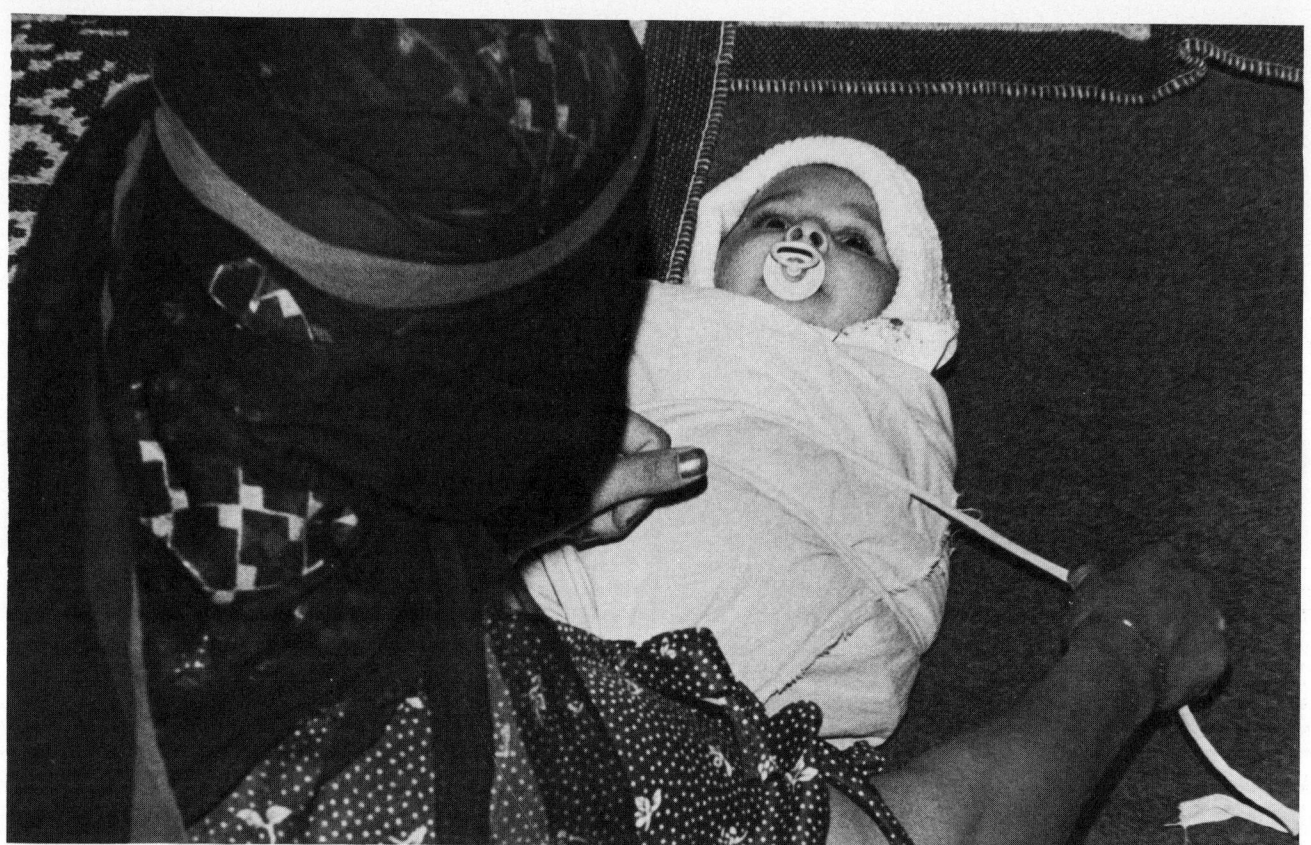

It is the custom to swaddle babies periodically during the first three or four months after birth.

Most Sana'ani babies are born at home, attended by female relatives or a midwife, and the mother remains in bed for a week following the birth. Then, every afternoon for the next forty days, she dresses in finery, often with a headdress much like the *taj*, and receives visitors from a raised couch in the *mafraj*. The couch is spread with wool blankets and silk embroidered pillows, and the walls behind it are decorated with strings of colored electric lights, tapestry purses containing the Koran, and herbs symbolizing happiness and fertility. Women may be hired to chant from the Koran, and a special party on the fortieth day marks the end of the new mother's seclusion.

If the child is a boy, he is circumcised on the seventh day. A breakfast party may follow, either for the family or for the father and his male relatives and friends, and for which chanters are hired to read the Koranic texts relating the childhood of the Prophet Muhammad.

The dead of Sana'a are usually buried before sundown on the day of death. The body is washed and shrouded in a prescribed manner by a holy man or close relative, viewed by the family and taken to the mosque, where a special prayer might be offered. A procession of male chanters, some hired, accompany the deceased to the cemetery, giving alms in his name along the way. The Koran is read during the burial, and the site is marked only by plain gravestones or, more frequently, by a simple pile of rocks.

The general period of mourning is ten days, during which women friends, dressed in black, come to join in chanting from the Koran. A widow remains in seclusion for forty days after her husband's death.

The austerity of gravesites is contradictory to the significance of Islamic burial, a triumphant and natural return to the revered earth.

Sana'a is a developing, expanding city which retains
its uniqueness in an intriguing blend of old and new.

'Abd Al-Wahhab and Azizah

'Abd al-Wahhab, a soft-spoken, bespectacled young man of twenty-eight and Azizah, a shy, elfin-faced girl of nineteen, were married through an arrangement between their families. 'Abd al-Wahhab works in Sana'a, and the couple lives in a rented house in the Old Town, several hours from their village home. Only their ten-month-old son, Tariq, and 'Abd al-Wahhab's brother, who is a student at Sana'a University, live with them.

'Abd al-Wahhab went to a religious school in his village before attending secondary school in Sana'a. He has a bachelor's degree from a university in Cairo. Azizah had attended school for nine years when her parents informed her that she was to be married.

'Abd al-Wahhab's father gave him some money toward the dowry of 25,000 *riyal*s set by Azizah's parents, and 'Abd al-Wahhab worked and saved from his salary for three years to pay the rest. Azizah's father gave her a *mahr* of 5,000 *riyal*s, which she used to buy gold and new dresses for her wedding.

Though the couple are second cousins, they did not know each other before their marriage. Azizah laughingly admits that she had managed, before the wedding, to catch glimpses of 'Abd al-Wahhab from behind windows and doors when he came to lunch with her father, but 'Abd al-Wahhab did not see his bride's face until the night of their wedding. Both young people were very apprehensive during the pre-nuptial parties and celebrations.

Now, after two years of happy marriage, they can laugh at those fears, for they have grown to love each other very much. Their affection is demonstrated in a ready willingness to praise, help or simply be with the other. Even when Tariq was born, 'Abd al-Wahhab stayed at Azizah's side, breaking tradition and shocking his mother-in-law, who came from the village to help.

While 'Abd al-Wahhab works in his office in the morning, Azizah takes care of Tariq and cleans the house. A small, frail girl, she admits she finds it difficult to manage a home without an extended household of women to share the chores. She bakes bread in the *tannur* every other day and washes all the family's clothes by hand. When he returns from work, 'Abd al-Wahhab sometimes lends a hand in the preparation of the mid-day meal, especially when there are guests, but he confesses, "In this kitchen, I make many mistakes." With Tariq in his arms, he usually just offers encouragement from the doorway while Azizah kneads, stirs and grinds.

'Abd al-Wahhab spends the afternoon at home, chewing *qat* only on special occasions. Azizah doesn't go to *tafritah*s because she doesn't smoke the *mada'ah* or chew *qat* and, since 'Abd al-Wahhab is at home, she prefers to be with him. Sometimes they go together to family gatherings in the homes of relatives who live in the city, or Azizah visits a nearby aunt who is teaching her to sew.

'Abd al-Wahhab goes out occasionally in the evening to play chess with friends or to do the family's shopping. He goes to the mosque several times a week, and always attends Friday noon sermon at the Great Mosque, which is not far from his house. Azizah prays at home.

'Abd al-Wahhab feels that he is very lucky to have a loving, obedient wife like Azizah. He has friends whose lives have been ruined by bad marriages arranged for them by their parents and that, he says, is very sad. "Arranged marriages are our custom, and they are a good way, but the parents must know the other family and take the time to choose wisely for their children."

Azizah places her hand on his shoulder and nods in solemn agreement.

There is a lasting fascination for all those who come to know Sana'a, city of contrast.

Glossary

bint al-sahn
a yeast or baking powder bread topped with honey and served as a first course

futah
gathered, calf-length skirt worn by Yemeni men

hajj
pilgrimage to Mecca; one who has made the pilgrimage is known as al-Hajj

hammam
public bath house

henna
reddish brown dye from the leaves of the *henna* plant

hilbah
a whipped fenugreek dip, sometimes flavored with hot sauce or herbs, and served in meat broth

imam
Muslim leader descended from the Prophet Muhammad who exercises spiritual and temporal leadership

jambiyah
curved dagger

ka'bah
small stone building in the courtyard of the Great Mosque at Mecca that contains a sacred black stone

khubz
circular, flat loaves of wheat bread

lithmah
rectangular scarf which Sana'ani women wrap around their heads in such a fashion that it can be pulled up to cover all but the eyes

mada'ah
waterpipe

mafraj
living room, usually on the uppermost level of the house, which is furnished with floor cushions and provides views of city and landscape

maghmuq
black cloth, tie-dyed in red and white, used by Sana'ani women as a face veil with the *sitarah*

mahr
the bride's portion of the dowry

makhbazah
a rounded pillow attached to a flat straw surface which is used to shape *khubz*

maluj
circular, flat loaves of wheat bread, larger than *khubz* and made with fenugreek

mashaddah
large square of cloth which Yemeni men wrap into a turban

mazhagah
grindstone

mu'adhdhin
the functionary who performs the call to prayer

naqsh
designs applied to hands and feet by dotting black dye on the skin with a small stick

qat
a mild, non-addictive plant of the coffee family which grows in Yemen and is chewed by many Yemenis for afternoon entertainment and relaxation

qishr
weak drink made by steeping coffee bean husks in boiling water with cinnamon, cloves and ginger

riyal
unit of Yemeni currency equivalent to US $.22

sailah
riverbed for seasonal rainfall that flows from the mountains southeast of Sana'a

samsarah
inn/warehouse where caravans rested for the night and where goods were inspected, taxed and stored

shafut
a maize pancake soaked in sour milk and spiced with thyme, mint, spring onions and parsley

shaikh
headman or tribal chief

sharshaf
ankle-length black skirt and black cape to which is attached a full-face black veil; fashionable among Sana'ani women as an outer garment, an alternative to the *sitarah*

shubbak
window box on exterior wall of houses where foods are kept cool; also, latticed window through which women can peer without being seen

sitarah
large red and blue square of batik material with which Sana'ani women cover themselves when they go out

suq
market

tabinah
co-wife

tafritah
women's afternoon visit

taj
bridal headdress

tannur
cylindrical earthenware oven

zahawiq
spicy sauce of tomatoes, garlic, salt, cumin, red pepper and mint

Selected References

Ansell, Christine
Notes on Food Classification In Yemen
USAID, Sana'a
1978

Budd, Jack
Studies on Islam, a Simple Outline of the Islamic Faith
Red Sea Mission Team
Great Britain
1975

Costa, Pablo and Ennio Vicario
Yemen, Land of Builders
Academy Editions
7 Holland Street, London W8
1977

Fayein, Claudie
Yemen
Petite Planete, Seuil
27 rue Jacob, Paris
1975

Kay, Henry Cassels
Yemen, Its Early Medieval History
Edward Arnold, publisher to the India Office
London, 1892

Kirkman, James, Editor
City of Sana'a
Museum of Mankind, Ethnography Dept. of the British Museum
World of Islam Festival Publishing Co. Ltd.
Middle East Centre, Cambridge
1976

Makhlouf, Carla
Changing Veils, Women and Modernization in North Yemen
University of Texas Press, Austin
1979

Myntti, Cynthia
Women and Development in Yemen Arab Republic
German Agency for Technical Cooperation, Ltd.
Eschborn, Federal Republic of Germany
1979

Myrop, Richard F.
Area Handbook for the Yemens
Superintendent of Documents
US Government Printing Office
Washington, D.C. 20402
1977

Scott, Hugh
In the High Yemen
Bradford and Dickens
London, 1942

Shankland Cox Partnership
Sana'a, A Report to UNESCO
16 Bedford Square, London
1978

Stookey, Robert W.
Yemen, The Politics of the Yemen Arab Republic
Westview Special Studies of the Middle East
Westview Press, Boulder, Colorado
1978

Swanson, Rebecca L.
Role of Women in the YAR
USAID, Sana'a
September, 1975

Tarcici, Adnan
The Queen of Sheba's Land
Nowfel Publishers, Beirut

Wenner, Manfred W.
Modern Yemen 1918–1966
Johns Hopkins Press
Baltimore, Maryland
1967

This book was composed by Brushwood Graphics, Ltd. in Quadritek Palatino text and display from a design by Janet Innes and Robin Hettleman. It was printed by Publication Press, Inc. on 70 pound Mead Offset Enamel and bound in Roxite A.